SIMPLIFY

A Life Anchored in Purpose

SUE ANN CORDELL

I want to hear from you. Please send your comments about this Bible Study to Sue Ann Cordell at sueann@shineworthy.com. Thank you!

SHINEWORTHY LIFESTYLES
A Positive Approach to Life!
www.shineworthy.com | sueann@shineworthy.com

SIMPLIFY

SECOND EDITION

ACKNOWLEDGEMENTS

I wish to thank all the following individuals for their love and support:

To my husband Randy who encouraged me to continue moving ahead at times when I wanted to give up. You inspire me in my walk with Christ through your unwavering example. I love you. To Becky – my graphic designer. Your enthusiasm and confidence have kept me focused. You have a gift of taking my random ideas and molding them into one concept that makes sense. What a talent you are! To my editor and friend Susan who used her talents and abilities to go over every word on every page. You did an incredible job, and I am filled with gratitude for you. To my son Bobby and Michelle who showed genuine interest in the project. To my daughter Hether and Rustin who allow me to bounce ideas off of them anytime, day or night. To my mother Lois and her daily prayers. Thank you for being my biggest cheerleader. And God. This is all for your glory. I am humbled by your unconditional love, and grateful for the blessings you so richly pour out on each of us daily. I am blessed to have you all in my life!

TABLE OF CONTENTS

SIMPLIFY INTRODUCTION

- Do you feel that your life is out of control?

- Do you feel frazzled?

- Do you feel overwhelmed?

- Do you avoid opening closet doors for fear of an avalanche?

- Do you hide when someone shows up at your house unexpectedly?

- Do you find yourself falling asleep during your favorite television show due to exhaustion?

- Do you find yourself digging through the dryer, looking for socks and underwear most every morning for someone in the family?

- Do your children have the number for Pizza Delivery memorized?

- Do you find yourself running late most of the time?

- Do you receive late notices in the mail because you forgot to pay the bills?

If you answered, "yes" to one or more of these questions, you are not alone. Most of us feel that every hour is a rush hour and we are missing out on the things in life that are truly important. Over the next six weeks, we will look into God's word and discover ways to change habits, re-prioritize, set goals, and begin to experience a simpler way of life.

New patterns of doing things, new thought habits, new ways of feeling must come slowly if they are to be maintained. Often it takes repeated reminders before these foreign behaviors become a part of our lives. It has been said that in order to change a habit or to accomplish a lifestyle change, you must practice it for at least six weeks. Over the next six weeks, we will work together to make the necessary changes that will allow you to get your life back under control.

I encourage you to take time each day to complete the assigned lesson and to make every effort to attend the group sessions once a week. There is no better, simpler plan for your life than the one God has for you. God created you to experience a better way—a life anchored in simplicity, contentment, joy, and rest.

Sue Ann Cordell

WEEK 1

A LIFE ANCHORED IN SIMPLICITY

Do you remember the song "Row, Row, Row Your Boat"? In that song, the first verse says, "Row, row, row your boat, gently down the stream. Merrily, merrily, merrily, merrily, life is but a dream." There have been days when I have felt just the opposite. Instead of rowing "gently" down the stream, I was fighting against the currents all day long. There was nothing "merrily" about my day, and life was more like a nightmare than a dream. Can you relate?

What can we do to get back to a simpler lifestyle? In this first unit of study, we will begin to look into God's word for basic principles that will guide us through baby steps that will enable us to slow down, try new things, change bad habits, find solitude, and even have time for some fun in the kitchen.

Anticipate all God wants to teach you this week! Ask Him to show you the things He wants you to see everyday as you study His word. Be open to a fresh and new approach to life!

DAY 1
Minutes and
Hours

DAY 2
New Ways

DAY 3
Make It a
Habit

DAY 4
Inner Quiet

DAY 5
Making it Fun

DAY 1
MINUTES AND HOURS

VERSES FOR THE DAY
Teach us to realize the brevity of life, so that we may grow in wisdom.
Psalm 90:12 (NLT)

For everything there is a season, a time for every activity under heaven.
Ecclesiastes 3:1 (NLT)

Several years ago, I worked in the banking industry. I had the opportunity to work in different departments. In the Bookkeeping Department, I processed canceled checks. Once a check was canceled, there was nothing else to be done in the process. The transaction was complete and could not be changed. I then moved into a Teller position. My main responsibility was to handle large sums of cash wisely and to keep everything balanced throughout the day, with every transaction. The final department that I worked in was the Loan Department. I processed applications, processed all of the paperwork and assisted in the loan closings. The most important piece of paperwork was the promissory note. This was the document that the customer was required to sign stating that they promised to pay back the entire sum of money that was borrowed.

How are you spending your time each day? Are you dwelling on the past? There is nothing you can do about the past. So many times we spend time trying to figure out ways to undo events that took place years ago or just yesterday. We worry and get stuck in the world of "if only". **Yesterday is like a canceled check – there is nothing you can do to change it.** Are you so caught up in your plans for the future that you fail to enjoy the present? There are people that are so driven to climb the corporate ladder that they are neglecting the things in life that really matter, such as family, friends, God, church. **Tomorrow is a promissory note – there is no guarantee that we will be granted another day.** The only time that we know we have is TODAY. What kind of choices are you making today? **Today is cash – spend it wisely!**

Do you find yourself running late most of the time?

In chapter four of the book entitled, "Messie No More", Sandra Felton deals with the issue of wasting time. She writes about a woman who always thinks she will be on time, but it doesn't ever seem to work out that way. She always underestimates how long it takes to do things. For twenty years it has taken her an hour to get ready for work in the morning. Nevertheless, every morning she optimistically thinks she can cut the time to forty-five minutes if she just hurries a little bit, so she sleeps an extra fifteen minutes. But every morning for twenty years she has been fifteen minutes late for work. Because she is always running late, she never has time to put the breakfast dishes in the dishwasher, straighten the bathroom, or hang up the clothes she decided not to wear. Sandra calls this one of the classic characteristics of a "Time Waster".

List some factors that cause you to waste time. Give examples of how they affect your life.

_____

_____

_____

What would you do if you had a couple of extra hours each day to use in any way you please?

Work requires at least eight hours each day, your family takes another large chunk, and chores, social obligations and exercise can consume the rest. There have been times in my life that I just wanted to scream out to the world... "Hey, I have nothing left to give, leave me alone!" What would you do if you had a couple of extra hours each day to use in any way you please?

_____

_____

_____

THOUGHT FOR THE DAY
Every hour and minute of your day belongs to you. Your schedule and your life are as simple or complicated as you decide.

HUMOR FOR THE DAY
A physician was driving her four-year-old daughter to preschool. She had left her stethoscope on the car seat, and her little girl picked it up and began playing with it. "Be still, my heart," thought the doctor. "My daughter wants to follow in my footsteps!" Then the child spoke into the instrument, "Welcome to McDonald's. May I take your order?"

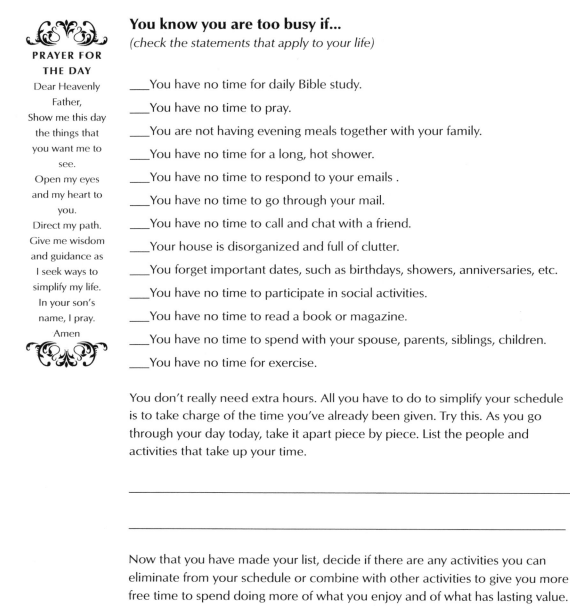

You know you are too busy if...

(check the statements that apply to your life)

____You have no time for daily Bible study.

____You have no time to pray.

____You are not having evening meals together with your family.

____You have no time for a long, hot shower.

____You have no time to respond to your emails .

____You have no time to go through your mail.

____You have no time to call and chat with a friend.

____Your house is disorganized and full of clutter.

____You forget important dates, such as birthdays, showers, anniversaries, etc.

____You have no time to participate in social activities.

____You have no time to read a book or magazine.

____You have no time to spend with your spouse, parents, siblings, children.

____You have no time for exercise.

You don't really need extra hours. All you have to do to simplify your schedule is to take charge of the time you've already been given. Try this. As you go through your day today, take it apart piece by piece. List the people and activities that take up your time.

_____

_____

Now that you have made your list, decide if there are any activities you can eliminate from your schedule or combine with other activities to give you more free time to spend doing more of what you enjoy and of what has lasting value.

_____

_____

_____

"As you go through each day, take time to treat everyone with dignity and respect and find some humor in the day!"
Sue Ann Cordell

DAY 2
NEW WAYS

Your decision to simplify your life will mean tampering with your comfort zone. It will mean relaxing your grip on the old and letting God help you discover the new. It will mean accepting challenges in every area of your life. In a word, it will mean change.

If you were to ask me about the best job I ever had, I would have to say the job of Piano Teacher. I loved taking brand new beginners and watching them transform into experienced, accomplished pianists. I enjoyed giving them the challenge of a new piece of music and coaching them on ways to complete the task. I observed children and adults gain confidence in their abilities, not only in piano skills, but also in other areas of their life. Simply by stepping out of their comfort zone and trying new things, they learned very quickly that if they set a goal and worked hard, they could reach their goals.

Not every student was that motivated, however. I did have some who wanted every lesson and every piece of music to be easy. Their only goal was to get the lesson over with so they could get on with other things. They did not practice and only showed up for the lessons because someone else wanted them to learn to play the piano. Their heart was not in it.

Change comes only when we really want to be changed. You can change, but you must want it. Change isn't always easy, but when God's hand is in it, it is always beneficial.

VERSES FOR THE DAY

Great is his faithfulness; his mercies begin afresh each morning. I say to myself, "The Lord is my inheritance; therefore, I will hope in him!" Lamentations 3:23-24 (NLT)

Don't copy the behavior and customs of this world, but let God transform you into a new person by changing the way you think. Then you will learn to know God's will for you, which is good and pleasing and perfect. Romans 12:2 (NLT)

Create in me a clean heart, O God. Renew a loyal spirit within me. Psalm 51:10 (NLT)

Trust in the Lord with all your heart; do not depend on your own understanding. Seek his will in all you do, and he will show you which path to take. Proverbs 3:5-6 (NLT)

There was a
religious lady
that had to do a
lot of traveling
for her business.
Flying made her
very nervous, so
she always took
her Bible along
with her to read
as it helped relax
her on the long
flights. One time,
she was sitting
next to a man.
When he saw
her pull out her
Bible, he gave a
little chuckle and
a smirk and went
back to what
he was doing.
After awhile, he
turned to her and
asked, "You don't
really believe
all that stuff in
there do you?"
The lady replied,
"Of course I do.
It is the Bible".
He said, "Well,
what about that
guy that was
swallowed by
that whale?" She
replied, "Oh,
Jonah. Yes, I
believe that, it is
in the Bible." He
asked, "Well how
do you suppose
he survived all
that time inside
the whale?" The
lady said, "Well,
I don't really

DO YOU HAVE THE WANT TO?

Do you feel that your life is out of control? Do you feel frazzled? Do you feel overwhelmed? Check the areas of your life that are making you feel out of control, frazzled, or overwhelmed.

___Finances ___Marriage ___Job ___Children

___Friendships ___Housework ___Weight ___Time Management

___Smoking ___Alcohol ___Health ___Gossip

___Spiritual Life ___Anger ___Self Image ___Parent

I've heard people say that if you want to change, you have to be more disciplined. Personally, I think discipline can only be a factor in achievement when you are in a structured program. There are programs that require you to do certain things in order to succeed. An example of this is the Piano Student that gets up every morning and practices before school because Mom makes them. They learn the songs and do well on lesson day because they don't want to get in trouble. If Mom is out of town, they don't practice and on lesson day, it shows. As long as people can remain in the disciplined program, they see improvements, but for some (me included), when the program ends, the old way of life takes over once again.

What about Willpower? I've heard people say that they couldn't change because they had no willpower. Quotes such as "Where there is a will there is a way" doesn't help if you already feel your life is out of control. It just causes confusion and guilt. Years ago, I attended a Baby Shower at a beautiful new home. The home was so new that the yard was not completely finished and the ground was still very soft. When it was time to leave I saw that cars were blocking me on the driveway, and instead of disturbing the other guests I decided to drive off of the driveway and into the yard. As soon as the wheels touched down, I knew I had made a terrible mistake. I immediately felt the car sinking into the ground. I tried turning the wheels and pressing slightly on the gas pedal, but the more I tried to move, the worse it got. Mud was covering everyone and everything in sight. The freshly seeded yard was completely torn up. Other women saw what was happening and tried to help. I finally swallowed my pride and went inside to tell the hostess what was going on. She called her husband to come home and help. He tried to get the car out, but it continued to get worse. A towing service had to be called to assist. The car, covered in mud, was finally pulled out. It left a huge hole in the yard, but after many months the lawn was restored to its original beauty. I was determined to change the situation, to make it better. Even though I had the willpower, I could not fix the problem.

Instead of discipline and willpower, you need focus. Most of us only want things to be better in a foggy sort of way. If you are able to focus on what it is that you want to do, then you will begin to change automatically. The discipline and willpower will come if they are needed.

I have never been known for my great photography skills. As a matter of fact, most of the pictures I have taken through the years have my finger or the strap of the camera included. If you didn't know my family well, and were just looking at pictures I have taken, you would think we were all born with half of a body, only part of a head or with very red eyes. But things are different for me now. We have a digital camera, and I love it! I don't even have to focus the picture. The camera does it for me. My fingers are never in the way, and the strap is so far from the frame that it is never included in the picture. Our family even looks normal in every shot that I take. Full bodies, normal shaped heads and you can even crop out things that you don't want included. Isn't modern technology wonderful and amazing?

With God's help you can see clearly and focus on the things that matter most! Write a brief prayer below, asking God to guide you as you focus on the simpler life you desire.

_____

_____

_____

Don't be afraid to step outside your comfort zone. Set personal goals, and ask God to help you meet those goals. If you try to do this on your own, you are setting yourself up for failure.

IN ORDER TO TAKE CARE OF OTHERS, YOU MUST FIRST TAKE CARE OF YOURSELF!

Feeling out of control? ___yes ___no

If you are not in control, what is controlling you?

_____

_____

know, I guess when I get to heaven, I will ask him." "What if he isn't in heaven?" The man asked sarcastically. "Then you can ask him," replied the lady.

For most people, losing control is a gradual process. I recommend taking **Baby Steps** in order to gain control of your life once again.

BABY STEPS

1. Identify three changes that you feel God is urging you to make in your life.

_____

_____

_____

2. Think of a specific area where you have resisted change.

_____

3. Identify one area of your work life where change could help you release stress.

_____

_____

4. Ask yourself what change you could make in your schedule that will provide you more time to spend with God.

_____

_____

DAY 3

MAKE IT A HABIT

In the late 70's, I served as vice president of an organization called Women of Atlanta Christian College. Most of the women in this organization were in their early to mid-twenties, newly married and taking on the role of "Pastor's Wife" for the first time. Because we wanted to glean from the experience of more mature women of faith, we often had guest speakers at our meetings. At one of our meetings, we were handed a pen and some paper and instructed to imagine what it would be like to have children and to write down the goals we would set for them. When we completed the exercise, the speaker asked this question, "Shouldn't the goals that you just wrote for your future children, be your goals right now?" Sometimes we need others to help us focus on what we want and to remind us that it is possible to obtain it.

It is never too late to start something new! Just because your life is chaotic today does not mean it has to be that way forever.

VERSES FOR THE DAY

Good planning and hard work lead to prosperity, but hasty shortcuts lead to poverty.
Proverbs 21:5 (NLT)

Don't copy the behavior and customs of this world, but let God transform you into a new person by changing the way you think. Then you will learn to know God's will for you, which is good and pleasing and perfect.
Romans 12:2 (NLT)

So think clearly and exercise self-control. Look forward to the gracious salvation that will come to you when Jesus Christ is revealed to the world. So you must live as God's obedient children. Don't slip back into your old ways of living to satisfy your own desires. You didn't know any better then. But now you must be holy in everything you do, just as God who chose you is holy.
I Peter 1:13-15 (NLT)

A Sunday school was teaching how God created everything, including human beings. Little Johnny seemed especially intent when they told him how Eve was created out of one of Adam's ribs. Later in the week his mother noticed him lying down as though he were ill, and said, "Johnny what is the matter?" Little Johnny responded, "I have a pain in my side. I think I'm going to have a wife."

Dig the well before you are thirsty. – Ancient Proverb

Good order is the foundation of all good things. – Edmund Burke

Using your imagination, describe what you actually want for your life if money, time, energy, and other problems were not a consideration.

_____

_____

_____

_____

What things in your daily routine produce a lack of focus? Put a check by the ones listed below that you can give up or do more moderately.

___job	___children's activities	___volunteer activities
___hobbies	___clutter	___lack of funds

In order to simplify and focus, certain habits need to be formed. A habit is something that we do so often that it becomes second nature. It is so much a part of our every day life that we don't even realize we are doing it.

At first the change may seem awkward, but in a short period of time through repetition it becomes a habit for you.

Are you right-handed or left-handed? _____

In the space below, write your name with the opposite hand than you usually use.

_____

Now write your name with the other hand.

_____

The awkwardness that you experienced when you wrote your name the first time is what it feels like to do something new for the first time. If you were to practice writing your name with this hand for several days, it would begin to feel natural to you. Forming new habits will be much the same.

With God's help, you can simplify your life by eliminating bad habits and forming some that are better for you. Philippians 4:13 says, For I can do everything through Christ, who gives me strength.

Use the space below to write a prayer asking God to help you as you begin to eliminate bad habits and form new ones.

_____

_____

_____

_____

_____

_____

I took a look at my closet last week and realized it was out of control. There were way too many clothes in there. I could not even cram a tiny metal hanger into the clutter. If I wanted to buy a new outfit, I would have to get rid of something because there simply was no room left in the closet. Something had to be done, so I began taking out anything that I did not plan to wear again and organizing everything else to make room for new things.

Imagine your life as a closet. Is it cluttered with things that you have no use for? Take inventory and decide what old habits you will replace with new habits.

THOUGHT FOR THE DAY

The earth as God created it is a masterpiece of organization. He must have known that order is an environment in which we would thrive.

From the list below, circle any new habits that you want to implement and cross out the ones you want to eliminate.

Old Way	New Way
No time for daily Bible study.	Bible Study is a daily priority.
No time for prayer.	Prayer is a daily priority.
No time for evening meals with the family.	Evening meals with the family are a priority not an exception.
No time for a long, hot shower.	Make time to pamper myself.
No time to respond to e-mails.	Respond to e-mails twice a week.
No time to go through the mail.	Sort, file, and discard mail daily.
No time to call and chat with a friend.	Make time to call a friend at least twice a week.
No time to organize or de-clutter the house.	An orderly household is a priority.
No time to remember important dates.	Check calendar daily and plan ahead.
No time to participate in social activities.	Make time for one social event per month.
No time to read a book or magazine.	Relaxation and self- improvement are a priority.
No time to spend with spouse, parents, siblings, children	Weekly Family Nights are a priority
No time to exercise.	Exercise for at least 30 minutes three times a week.

Simplify...

Use a day planner or a desk calendar to help you organize your activities.

Create a list of important addresses, phone numbers, and dates then keep it in a desk drawer where you can actually find it!

Designate a place for the mail, the car keys, important papers, and messages.

DAY 4
INNER QUIET

My mother used to have a picture hanging in her kitchen of a woman slouched over, holding a mop with a scowl on her face. Underneath the picture was a caption that read, "Deary is Weary." She often wore a t-shirt that had a head shot of a woman that looked very frazzled that read, "I only have one nerve left and you're getting on it!" Have you ever felt this way? Are there times when even the smallest interruption causes you to change from a pleasant person to a tyrant? Do you ever get to a point where you rant and rave and feel anger mounting inside? When toddlers begin to act like that, we make them take a nap. When older children throw temper tantrums, we insist that they go to their rooms until they have a change in their attitude. What makes us think that we should be treated any differently? Sometimes we just need to stop what we are doing and take a nap! Other times, we need to spend time alone with God.

Your quest to find a simpler life will be more quickly realized when you learn to appreciate solitude- time alone to sort through your thoughts and feelings. Solitude affords an opportunity to escape the busyness all around you and allows your heart to respond to the still, small voice of God.

VERSES FOR THE DAY

Before daybreak the next morning, Jesus got up and went out to an isolated place to pray.
Mark 1:35 (NLT)

"Be still, and know that I am God! I will be honored by every nation. I will be honored throughout the world."
Psalm 46:10 (NLT)

Then Jesus said, "Come to me, all of you who are weary and carry heavy burdens, and I will give you rest. Take my yoke upon you. Let me teach you, because I am humble and gentle at heart, and you will find rest for your souls. For my yoke is easy to bear, and the burden I give you is light."
Matthew 11:28-30 (NLT)

O Jacob, how can you say the Lord does not see your troubles? O Israel, how can you say God ignores your rights? Have you never heard? Have you never understood? The Lord is the everlasting God, the Creator of all the earth. He never grows weak or weary. No one can measure the depths of his understanding. He gives power to the weak and strength to the powerless. Even youths will become weak and tired, and young men will fall in exhaustion. But those who trust in the Lord will find new strength. They will soar high on wings like eagles. They will run and not grow weary. They will walk and not faint.
Isaiah 40:27-31 (NLT)

About 5,000 men were fed that day, in addition to all the women and children! Immediately after this, Jesus insisted that his disciples get back into the boat and cross to the other side of the lake, while he sent the people home. After sending them home, he went up into the hills by himself to pray. Night fell while he was there alone.
Matthew 14:21-23 (NLT)

A little boy
opened the
big and old
family Bible
with fascination,
and looked at
the old pages
as he turned
them. Suddenly,
something fell
out of the Bible,
and he picked it
up and looked at
it closely. It was
an old leaf from
a tree that had
been pressed
in between the
pages. "Momma,
look what I
found," he called
out. " What have
you got there,
dear?" his mother
asked. With
astonishment
in the young
boy's voice, he
answered: "I think
it's Adam's suit!"

**THOUGHT
FOR THE DAY**
Time alone with
God helps you
to stay focused
on the basics and
to shake off the
things that have
no lasting value.

In the rush of your busy life, finding time for solitude may seem like an impossible dream. The answer is to determine to make room for it, just as Jesus did.

Write a prayer to God asking him to show you ways to find solitude in the midst of your busy schedule.

_____

_____

_____

At least two times a year, I take time off from work simply to spend a full day in solitude with God. I call these "Mental Health Days". I highly recommend this for you too! If you have young children at home, ask a friend to watch them for a day. Offer to return the favor so that she too can have a day of solitude.

When your mind begins to feel overwhelmed, solitude will work for you, just as it did for Jesus. You need time to sort through and unload those thoughts and images that distract you. You need time to reconnect with God and focus again on the simple, basic principles he has called you to live by.

When my daughter was three years old, a friend of mine had agreed to watch her while I went with my husband to make some hospital visits. In addition to watching my daughter, she was keeping two other children. The children were playing very well together so Judy decided to run to the restroom for a minute. She had just closed the door, took a deep sigh and my daughter began knocking on the door and yelling, "Miss Judy, I know you're in there. Come out now or I'll call the Police!" When there are small children around, it can be difficult to find time for solitude. If you are able to stay at home with your children, insist that they have a quiet time so that you can have your quiet time!

Schedule a regular time each day to be alone with God. Don't just assume you will find time. If you haven't planned it ahead of time, it may never happen.

Ask God to help you learn to recognize your limits and to catch a few minutes alone before you reach overload.

Make a list of places at home or at work where you can be alone.

_____

_____

_____

_____

_____

DAY 5
MAKING IT FUN

**VERSES FOR
THE DAY**

Give thanks to
the Lord, for he is
good! His faithful
love endures
forever.
Psalm 118:1 (NLT)

"So don't worry
about these
things, saying,
'What will we
eat? What will we
drink? What will
we wear?' These
things dominate
the thoughts of
unbelievers, but
your heavenly
Father already
knows all your
needs. Seek
the Kingdom
of God above
all else, and live
righteously, and
he will give you
everything you
need.
Matthew 6:31-33
(NLT)

Don't worry
about anything;
instead, pray
about everything.
Tell God what you
need, and thank
him for all he has
done. Then you
will experience
God's peace,
which exceeds
anything we can
understand. His
peace will guard
your hearts and
minds as you live
in Christ Jesus.
Philippians 4:6-7
(NLT)

I was in St. Augustine, Florida recently and purchased a "Life is good®" t-shirt. I love my shirt and wear it often. It is a great reminder to me that life really is good. Instead of focusing on the negatives, I now realize that for the Christian, the positives far outweigh the negatives. Bert and John Jacobs created the "Life is good®" company in 1994. For five years they slept in their van, lived on PB&J, and sold t-shirts door-to-door in college dorms. Then one day with a combined sum of $78 in the bank, they created Jake (a character with a big smile), and he showed them the way.

These days, Jake and "Life is good®" have spread optimism nationwide. On the tag of my shirt it reads, ***"do what you like and like what you do."*** What a great message!

Take time today to pay attention to the good and positive things in your life. Celebrate the blessings that God has given to you and your family. Clear off a counter in your kitchen, and make some cookies. If you don't have time to bake, then try the recipe included at the end of this unit. It is delicious and requires no baking! Play your favorite music. Watch a funny movie.

List other ideas for living the life out of this day:

_____

_____

_____

_____

_____

_____

_____

And now, dear brothers and sisters, one final thing. Fix your thoughts on what is true, and honorable, and right, and pure, and lovely, and admirable. Think about things that are excellent and worthy of praise. Philippians 4:8

Simple living enables you to have a good time on a very low budget. Look for activities that are free. Make a sincere effort to spend quality time, as well as quantity time, with the people that matter most to you. If you feel a frown coming over your face, change it to a smile.

If you are sick and tired of being sick and tired then do something about it! With God's help you can live a simpler life.

I don't know about you, but I want to slow down. I want to quit moving so fast. I want to look for fun and just feel groovy! Hey, that would make a great song!

TODAY'S RECIPE

NO BAKE COOKIES
(A favorite at my house!)

2 cups of sugar
½ cup of milk
½ cup of peanut butter
6 oz package of chocolate morsels
2½ cups of raw quick oats
1 stick of butter
½ teaspoon of vanilla

Boil sugar, milk, chocolate and butter for 1½ minutes. Remove from heat and add remaining ingredients. Drop from spoon onto wax paper. Let dry and serve.

GROUP SESSION

WEEK 1

MOVE OUT THE CLUTTER AND MAKE ROOM FOR GOD

I.   For _____ there is a season, a _____ for every activity
     under heaven. Ecclesiastes 3:1

     The time to simplify is _____. The time to get rid of the _____
     is now.

     Definition of closet – n. a small cabinet, compartment or room for storage.
     Definition of clean – adj. Free from impurities, dirt, or contamination; neat.

II. _____ is a selfish desire to acquire more than one needs or
     deserves. A person that is greedy is never satisfied with what they have.
     They always want more. They are so busy making money so they can have
     more stuff, bigger houses, better cars, get a better job, and on and on it
     goes.

     Problem: Little or no time for God, family, or friends.

III. _____ is knowing that you have done something wrong and you feel
     the need to hide it. Women tend to feel _____ guilt.

     "But those who do what is _____ come to the light so others can
     see that they are doing what _____ wants." John 3:21.

IV. _____ is often malicious talk; a person who spreads
     sensational or intimate facts.

     So be careful how you _____, Don't live like fools, but like those who
     are _____. Ephesians 5:15

WEEK 2

A LIFE ANCHORED IN THE RIGHT DIRECTION

My husband and I have been lost in some of the most interesting places in the world. In 1987 we had the privilege of going to Hong Kong. We went with a group from Chevrolet and were supposed to stick with the group at all times. Being the adventuresome couple that we are, we decided that we would get off of the beaten path and take our own tour. As my husband often says, "we need to take the scenic route". We were having a good time exploring the sights and learning more about the culture around us. Dinner at the hotel was to be at a certain time for the group, and we realized that we needed to make our way back in time for the evening events. We thought it would be quite simple to hail a cab, then show the driver a book of matches from the hotel, and get back to our original destination in a reasonable fashion. What we did not count on was the fact that we did not speak the language, and we did not understand the proper procedures for hailing a cab in Hong Kong. After numerous times of calling out and attempting to wave down a cab, we decided it might be best to try to find our way on foot. Not a good idea. We tried once again to hail a taxi, and a kind police officer finally had pity on us and explained through sign language that in order for a cab driver to pick up a passenger, one must stand inside the marked off area of the street that is designated for passenger pick up. His sign language was more like pushing us along the street and pointing to the marked off area. Once we stepped inside the box and waved when a cab came by, the driver pulled right up and took us to the hotel. This was one of our most memorable adventures. I could spend days writing about times that we have been lost.

The key to reaching your destination is to know where you are going and how you will get there.

In this second unit of study, we will discover ways to simplify by looking into God's word and setting our sights on the good results. I have found that if I don't know where I am going, I will not know when I have arrived. We will learn ways to map out a plan, set goals, and focus on the things that matter most in our lives.

Anticipate all God wants to teach you this week! Ask Him to show you the things He wants you to see everyday as you study His word. Be open to a fresh and new approach to life!

DAY 1
God's
Purpose

DAY 2
Saying No

DAY 3
Lighten the
Load

DAY 4
The Signs
Along the
Way

DAY 5
Making it Fun

DAY 1
GOD'S PURPOSE

So whether we are here in this body or away from this body, our goal is to please him.
2 Corinthians 5:9 (NLT)

So we don't look at the troubles we can see now; rather, we fix our gaze on things that cannot be seen. For the things we see now will soon be gone, but the things we cannot see will last forever.
2 Corinthians 4:18 (NLT)

If we live, it's to honor the Lord. And if we die, it's to honor the Lord. So whether we live or die, we belong to the Lord.
Romans 14:8 (NLT)

"For I know the plans I have for you," says the Lord." They are plans for good and not for disaster, to give you a future and a hope.
Jeremiah 29:11 (NLT)

God has a plan and purpose for your life- a purpose that fits perfectly with the gifts and talents he has placed in you. When your goals are in harmony with God's plan, your life is bound to be simpler and happier. The concept that God has created you with a specific purpose in mind may make perfect sense to you, and yet you wonder how to identify and get into step with that purpose.

Set a goal to spend time getting to know your Creator. Choose a time each day to read a chapter from the New Testament. Soon you will begin to understand more about who God is and his overall intentions for humankind. Spend time in prayer daily. Pray while you are waiting in traffic, walking, in the car-pool line after school, or as you wait for soccer practice to end.

Next, set a goal to spend time learning more about yourself. God has placed gifts and talents in your life—some are obvious and some are just waiting to be discovered. Make a list of activities and tasks you are good at and enjoy. What makes you feel happy and motivated?

_____

_____

_____

As you discover more about God and more about yourself, you will find it easier to set goals that are consistent with who you really are and what you are meant to do and be.

BABY STEPS FOR GOAL SETTING

1. Determine what you want right now.

_____

_____

2. Describe what it looks like.

_____

_____

3. In order to change a negative into a positive, describe the feelings you have right now. What can you do to change your negative feelings into positive feelings?

_____

_____

4. You have to be determined to change and want it really bad. Do you want it bad enough to change?

_____

_____

5. Get to the core.
Why do you want to change? _____

Why do you want to simplify? _____

Why does it matter? _____

In order to reach a goal and maintain it, there must be meaning, purpose and desire.

When you are tempted to stay the way you are, remember the feelings you have and remember why you want to change!

Manning a speed
trap one day, I
stopped a young
woman and told
her she was going
15 mph over
the speed limit.
"Yes, I know,"
she hurriedly
explained. "but
I'm very low on
gas and I'm trying
to reach the next
station before I
run out."

A MISSION STATEMENT

In business, corporations are instructed to develop a mission statement for their employees in order to set a standard by which to work. I want to challenge you to do this for your personal life. I have developed a mission statement, and it has enabled me to stay focused on my personal goals.

Write a brief prayer below asking God to help you write a mission statement for your life.

_____

_____

_____

God does not
have a wonderful
plan for your life.
He has something
far better – a
wonderful
purpose! –R. Paul
Steven

Take some time to work on your own mission statement. It may take a few days to put it in writing, and that is okay. The statement will also serve as a reminder of your goals and purpose at times when you feel like giving up. I highly recommend that you take the time this week to write your statement.

_____

_____

_____

_____

_____

_____

The key to simplifying your life in regard to goals is to set wise, clear, and attainable goals consistent with God's purpose for your life.

Setting goals and writing out a mission statement sounds great, but what about the days when every thing seems to go wrong? What about the times when you have one crisis after another? Well, if you have been proactive by setting goals and living by your mission statement, when a crisis strikes or something unexpected happens, the stress level is less likely to escalate.

John 16:33 says, " I have told you all this so that you may have peace in me. Here on earth you will have many trials and sorrows. But take heart, because I have overcome the world."

Setting goals and planning ahead will give you a means to an end. It's like seeing a light at the end of the tunnel. Set attainable goals that are specific and time phased.

When setting goals, be true to the vision God has given you- even if you only have one or two pieces of the puzzle.

PRAYER FOR THE DAY

Dear Heavenly Father,
I ask that you guide me as I write my mission statement today. Show me the things that you want me to see. Help me to set attainable goals and to trust in you completely. Give me wisdom as I seek ways to simplify my life. In your son's name, I pray. Amen.

DAY 2
SAYING NO

VERSES FOR THE DAY

"The eyes of the Lord watch over those who do right, and his ears are open to their prayers. But the Lord turns his face against those who do evil."
I Peter 3:12 (NLT)

I don't mean to say that I have already achieved these things or that I have already reached perfection. But I press on to possess that perfection for which Christ Jesus first possessed me. No, dear brothers and sisters, I have not achieved it, but I focus on this one thing: Forgetting the past and looking forward to what lies ahead, I press on to reach the end of the race and receive the heavenly prize for which God, through Christ Jesus, is calling us.
Philippians 3:12-14 (NLT)

So be careful how you live. Don't live like fools, but like those who are wise. Make the most of every opportunity in these evil days. Don't act thoughtlessly, but understand what the Lord wants you to do.
Ephesians 5:15-17 (NLT)

Most women are very capable of multi-tasking and doing many things well. Remember the lyrics to the song about how women can bring home the bacon and fry it up in the pan? We try to do it all, have it all, be all things to all people, fix everything, keep everyone happy, and in living this way, we tend to be exhausted most of the time.

One of my friends was living in Europe at the time of her 10th wedding anniversary. Her husband decided to do something really special and planned a surprise, romantic weekend get-away to Paris, France. He made arrangements for their children to stay with a friend, packed all of their clothes, made reservations at a romantic hotel, and showed up unexpectedly to swoop her away for the weekend of her dreams. It was like a fairy tale come true! My friend is like most women. She keeps a candle burning at both ends most of the time. She works a full-time job, serves on committees at church, actively participates in the church choir, and is the mother of two children. She was so excited and surprised when her husband appeared at her office door and said, "I'm here to take you away from everything for the weekend. We are going to Paris for a romantic get-away." So off they went.

When they arrived in Paris and checked into the hotel, they freshened up and went out for a lovely dinner and then back to the hotel for well.........let your imagination take you wherever you want to go from here. As soon as my friend's head hit the pillow, she fell fast asleep. She said she tried to stay awake, but could not. They were in Paris for two nights and three days and due to her exhaustion, she slept most of the time.

Even in doing good things, we can over commit. In order to take care of others, we must first take care of ourselves. One of the hardest things for a woman to say is "no".

Don't let the good things in life rob you of the best things. – Buster Rothman

In the space below, list all of your responsibilities, and activities. If you need extra space for this, feel free to write in the margins.

_____

_____

_____

_____

It can be difficult to say no to friends, family, coworkers, and others at church. But unless you do, other people's priorities will clutter your life and leave you with less time and energy to focus on what God wants from you. In setting and maintaining your priorities, you have to learn when to say no as well as when to say yes.

When you are asked to volunteer for something, think before you speak! Don't just say yes without considering how it will affect your goals. Take a look at the examples below and put a check by the ones that relate to you.

___Your boss asks you to spend another late night at the office. In saying yes to your boss, you have to say no to your son's soccer game.

___You agree to help with the school bake sale. In saying yes, you have to say no to prayer time with your Bible study group.

___You decide to take some classes at the local college in order to get a promotion at work. By saying yes to your career, you say no to story time with your kids.

Saying yes to too many good things could mean that you are saying no to your relationship with God. Even when your intentions are the best, those times of prayer, Bible reading, and quiet times of solitude can slip away in the rush of other activities. Other times, they can slip away into a deep sleep, due to exhaustion.

Take time to evaluate every new request, project, or activity based on how it will fit in with your priorities.

Two old ladies in a rest home were talking. One of them said to the other, "It's my birthday. I'm eighty years old and by George, I want to do something shocking. So, I'm going to run through the cafeteria naked today."

Sure enough, she runs through the cafeteria with nothing on.

Two men are eating sloppy joes, and they see her. One of them says to the other, "Say, Alma's jogging clothes are looking kinda wrinkled today, aren't they?"

Write a prayer to God, asking him to help you simplify your life and increase your sense of satisfaction with your decision to simplify.

_____

_____

_____

Prioritizing our life often means putting best things before good things and keeping first things in first place. In Matthew 6:33, Jesus urges his disciples to put God things first. When your relationship with God takes first place in your life, he will help you put order to the rest.

Seek the Kingdom of God above all else, and live righteously, and he will give you everything you need. Matthew 6:33

Here we are, two thousand years later and this same principle applies for us today!

One of the primary reasons that we say yes when we really should say no is to avoid conflict and guilt. But every time you say yes there will have to be a no. Ask God to guide you as you consider what he wants you to say in each circumstance. As you read the Bible and spend time talking to him in prayer, you will begin to see how all the other pieces of your life fit together. You will gain "God Confidence". Conflict will be replaced with peace, and guilt will be replaced with contentment.

In my mission statement, I state that I want to make an eternal difference with my life and in the lives of others. In order for me to fulfill this mission, I have to say no to some things that I would prefer to say yes to. Guilt creeps into my heart every once in a while, and I have to stop and assess the situation. If I truly believe that I am doing the things that God wants me to do, then I have no reason to feel guilty about it.

A minister's wife came to me with a concern about her involvement in the church activities. She attends a church of 700 members, and there is something going on every day and every night at the church. She felt very guilty because she could not participate in all of the activities, take care of her family, and do well at her full-time job. I asked her to list the things that she felt were most important for her to attend and what other priorities she had. In looking over her list, we saw several activities that she could eliminate in order to spend more time with her family. One of the best things that she did was make a decision to say no to any and all activities on Tuesdays in order to declare that night "Family Night". She had to say no to some good activities but said yes to the best ones for her life. I think after three years, her guilt is finally diminishing, and she feels comfortable telling others that Tuesday nights are always reserved for Family Night.

Guilt Free Recipe for Saying No

- Keep a desk calendar so that you can easily see how a request will fit into your schedule.
- Before adding something new to your schedule, decide what it will replace.
- If you know you can't take something on, say so on the spot.
- Schedule specific times for important relationships.
- When needed, simply say no; no excuse is necessary.

PRAYER FOR THE DAY

Dear Heavenly Father,
Teach me to count my days that I may gain a wise heart.
Help me to commit everything to you.
Give me the courage to say no when necessary and the wisdom to say yes when the time is right.
Help me to simplify my life so that I may experience a life of fulfillment in serving you.
In your son's name, I pray.
Amen

DAY 3
LIGHTEN THE LOAD

"Yes, a person is a fool to store up earthly wealth but not have a rich relationship with God."
Luke 12:21 (NLT)

"Don't store up treasures here on earth, where moths eat them and rust destroys them, and where thieves break in and steal. Store your treasures in heaven, where moths and rust cannot destroy, and thieves do not break in and steal. Wherever your treasure is, there the desires of your heart will also be.
Matthew 6:19-21 (NLT)

Then he said, "Beware! Guard against every kind of greed. Life is not measured by how much you own." Then he told them a story: "A rich man had a fertile farm that produced fine crops. He said to himself, 'What should I do? I don't have room for all my crops.' Then he said, 'I know! I'll tear down my barns and build bigger ones. Then I'll have room enough to store all my wheat and other goods. And I'll sit back and say to myself, "My friend, you have enough stored away for years to come. Now take it easy! Eat, drink, and be merry!"' "But God said to him, 'You fool! You will die this very night. Then who will get everything you worked for?
Luke 12:15–20 (NLT)

My grandmother used to tell me stories about her life experiences during the "Great Depression". It took place in this country many years ago. Her father was a very successful business owner and lost everything as a result of the economic crisis during that time. Fortunately, my grandmother had completed the Frances Nightingale School of Nursing and was able to work at the hospital in Johnson City, Tennessee. She was the only family member that had a job, and everyone depended on her for food, shelter, and clothing. After surviving such a horrible experience, she always felt the need to store canned goods in her cellar, meats in her smokehouse, clothes and shoes in every closet. At the age of 62, she was forced to retire. If mandatory retirement had not been in force at that time, she would have continued working. Not because she wanted to work, but because she was afraid that she might not survive if another economic depression were to strike.

I can understand why my grandmother felt this way, but for most of us, we hold on to our stuff for other reasons. We are experiencing "stuff overload" and life is everything but simple when this happens.

Consider how much stuff you have. Take a look at the POSSESSIONS LIST below. Put a check by any items that you possess.

___Storage Shed	___Basement
___Attic	___More than one Mower
___Ice Cream Freezer	___Once used Glue Gun
___Boxes of Jigsaw Puzzles	___Old Magazines
___Expired Coupons	___Old Purses
___Broken Furniture	___Plastic Flowers
___Boxed up Trophies	___Dead Tennis Balls
___Unmatched Socks	___Exercise Equipment
___Outdated Wardrobe	___Worn out Shoes
___Clothes that no longer fit	___Outdated Phone Books

___Unused Craft Supplies	___Old Pairs of Glasses	___Waffle Iron
___Bread Machine	___Tarnished Jewelry	___Bud Vases
___Cracked Flowerpots	___Dried up Pens	___Broken Toys
___Outdated Sale Papers		

This list could go on and on. It can be quite a chore to store and protect so many possessions. You have probably wondered why you do it or what you can do about it. It can be comforting to know you have something for every occasion. There just might be a time when you need a backup mower and the thoughts of knowing that you have one stored away brings comfort to the soul. And what about the wicker furniture that you stored in the attic when you bought the new sofa and chair? The pieces were too good to get rid of. Did I mention the bicycle helmet that hangs in the laundry room? You might decide to purchase a bike one day, and then you will need that helmet. Do you really think you will want to wear the clothes you haven't been able to wear since you gained thirty pounds if and when you get back down to that size?

The problem that we all face when we have so much stuff is that the volume and clutter begins to take over, and we no longer have control of the stuff. It has taken control of us!

Do you look at all your stuff and feel overwhelmed at the thoughts of clearing out the clutter? _____

Take a good look around you, give yourself a good talking to, and take charge. Set aside some time to take action. Donate those clothes to a charitable organization such as Goodwill, Salvation Army, or a Right To Life Thrift Store. Give those puzzles to a retirement center. Haul off all broken toys and furniture. Have a Yard Sale. When you take control of your stuff rather than allowing your stuff to take control of you. You will enjoy a wonderful freedom that enables you to simplify your life.

Write a prayer asking God to help you take charge and take time to lighten the load.

_____

_____

_____

HUMOR FOR THE DAY
A friend who is bald says he will never wear a turtleneck sweater. He's afraid he'll look like a roll-on deodorant!

This is the same friend who said he used to use Head & Shoulders—but now he needs Mop & Glow!

There is nothing wrong with having stuff, but when it becomes "stuff overload" it is very easy to lose sight of the important things in life. Things like spiritual growth and relationships with family and friends begin to suffer.

Unless you make an effort to control your accumulation of possessions, your possessions will eventually control you.

"Debt Overload" is another area that can really complicate life. My grandmother learned some valuable lessons about money as she experienced life during the Great Depression. She learned to live on less than she made. She learned to save for the things she wanted. Even though she worked hard for her money, she lived a simple life. My grandmother was an exceptional woman. She went through a divorce in the 40's, worked outside the home, and raised two boys as a single mother. She did all of this at a time when most women were looked down on for working outside the home. With all her heartaches and struggles, she never lost sight of the most important thing in her life. Her relationship with God was a top priority in her home. I thank God for her legacy, and I pass it on to you today.

THOUGHT FOR THE DAY
Freeing yourself of unneeded possessions will make it easier to utilize and enjoy the possessions you decide to keep.

There was a time in this country that if you needed a house, you built it. If you needed clothes, you made them. If you wanted bread, you baked it. Very few people live this way anymore. The problem is that we have taken things to the other extreme. If we need a house, we finance it for twenty or thirty years. If we need clothes, we charge them on a credit card. If we want bread, we pull out a debit card. We work hard for the things we have, but by the time we have them paid for, they are worn out or obsolete.

I saw a bumper sticker once that read, "I owe, I owe, so off to work I go." When we work just to pay the bills and continue to get deeper in debt, we find ourselves in "debt overload".

Living a Debt-Free Life will allow you to control your money instead of allowing your money to control you.

Mary Hunt is the creator of the Cheapskate Monthly Newsletter. She has this advice for you today:

It is never too late to start again. I couldn't possibly tell you how many times I fell flat on my financial face and had to start again. Actually, I could list those pitfalls, but it would be too embarrassing. Let me just say that for nearly 20 New Year's Eves in a row, my resolution was to get out of debt and fix my money problems.

Did I tell anyone? No. Did I follow through? That depends on what you mean by "follow through." If one week of not using a credit card counts, then the answer would be " a couple of times." I made the same promise year after year after year—and failed year after year after year.

My point is it doesn't matter now that I failed so many times. What matters is that I finally got it right.

I wish I could say that my New Year's resolution stuck on the first try. But that wasn't it at all. It was 1982 and my family was horribly in debt, just barely hanging on by our fingernails. In a last ditch effort, we attempted to become self-employed by joining a distribution organization that turned out to be a little more than a pyramid scam. That became our final plunge into the dark abyss of financial devastation. Unemployed and with our home ready to be foreclosed, we came to the end. There was no place to turn, no more credit to be had. The unsecured debt I'd amassed was in the six figures. Yeah, you read that right. And that's when I made a decision, a promise: I will do anything to pay back all of the debt and do whatever I must to change my horrible spendthrift ways.

We did pay back every single dime of that horrible debt, including all the interest and penalties. We did not lose our home; I never worked so hard in all my life! We did not claim bankruptcy. I became content as paying off debts energized me and kept me going. And now the joy and passion of my life is to encourage, teach and lead others to do the same.

It doesn't matter how many times you've tried in the past to stop your out-of-control spending, start saving and get out of debt. What matters now is that you know and believe with all your heart that you can get it right this time. You can get out of debt. You can build an emergency nest egg even while you are in debt. You can be prepared for the future.

(Mary Hunt is the author of "Debt-Proof Living". For more information, check out her website at www.cheapskatemonthly.com)

When paying off your debts, aggressively pay off the smallest ones first. You'll get a sense of accomplishment from getting those out of the way early.

If a person gets their attitude toward money straight, it will help straighten out almost every other area in their life. – Billy Graham

DAY 4
THE SIGNS ALONG THE WAY

VERSES FOR THE DAY

Finishing is better than starting. Patience is better than pride. Ecclesiastes 7:8 (NLT)

How wonderful to be wise, to analyze and interpret things. Wisdom lights up a person's face, softening its harshness Ecclesiastes 8:1 (NLT)

Rejoice in our confident hope. Be patient in trouble, and keep on praying. Romans 12:12 (NLT)

"On every level of life from housework to heights of prayer, in all judgment and all efforts to get things done, hurry and impatience are sure marks of an amateur."
–Evelyn Underhill

Patience is more than an aid to simplifying your life; it is a marker to help you measure your progress along the way. Maybe it is a small change that you notice. You no longer get angry when the person in front of you in the check out line is taking longer than you anticipated. You begin to tolerate things at work that used to make you angry. Things such as coworkers that take too long at the copier or repeatedly fail to fill the fax machine with paper.

Increased patience indicates that you are realizing that your job is just your job. You honor God by working hard, doing your best, and showing respect for your employer, but you are no longer driven to get ahead in pursuit of some flimsy, ambiguous standard. You have simplified your attitudes concerning your work.

Another indication that you are learning how to simplify your life is in the way you patiently wait for God's answers to your prayers.

You are changing from a frantically busy individual that is running so fast that you miss the true essence of life to a person who is each day growing more centered and balanced and living life as God intended.

Patience is exactly what it will take to reach your goal of a simpler life.

List how many times you have exercised patience in new ways this week.

_____

_____

_____

List some ways that you could use patience as a guide to your progress.

_____

_____

_____

God rejoices when he sees you walking in patience.

Write a prayer below, asking God to show you areas that you need to practice more patience.

_____

_____

_____

One sign of growth in this area of patience is your attitude toward children.

Psalm 127:3 says, *"Children are a gift from the LORD; they are a reward from him."*

Children need to feel loved and are longing for attention. In an effort to simplify your life, take some time to walk with a child, talk with a child, and hold them in your arms.

When I have a child come up to me, I always get on my knees to talk to them. This allows me to be at eye level with them. They are so precious, and I want to savor the moments that I have to spend with them.

One time my granddaughter was playing a guessing game with me. This was a game that she made up. She would hold on to the back of my legs, and I was to guess who was behind me. She would give me clues in order to help me with the answer. One day, she said, "Nana, guess who is behind you." I replied, "Oh, dear, I can't figure it out. I need a clue." This is the clue that she gave to me... "It is someone that you love very much that comes to your house every Sunday." Wow, this really touched me. She recognized that I was someone that loved her very much.

What is God like?...

God is cool. Awesome. Powerful, nice. Big, huge, wonderful, Loving, exciting, caring, giving and the Best!
– Adrienne, 8

God is very loving. I imagine He is very tall. I love him.
– Lauren, 9

God is like an apple. Apples look good on the outside and on the inside.
– Brandon, 10

God has big hands because He's got the whole world in His hands.
– Kalen, 9

I think he has a beard. He is not that old. He lives in heaven. Jesus is His son.
– Justin, 10

Take time to enjoy the innocence of a child. They can teach us a lot about life if we will just be patient and recognize the signs along the way.

Spending time with our families is essential to obtaining a simpler life. Some of my fondest memories as a child were times spent around the kitchen table with my parents. Some of my fondest memories of my children are times we have spent around the kitchen table. I am now at a point in my life where I get to create memories for my grandchildren, and I pray that one day they will say... "Some of my fondest memories are times spent around Nana's kitchen table."

What relationships do you need to make time for?

_____

_____

_____

_____

The things that are important to you will become priorities over everything else. One of my favorite things to do is to spend time with my husband. We have blocked one night a month as Date Night. We both know that on the fourth Thursday of the month, we do something together, just for fun, romance, and adventure. This is not a night to discuss our finances, family issues, etc. It is a DATE! When you are dating, you go out just for fun, and after years of marriage, we still enjoy going out with each other simply as Randy and Sue Ann. There are twelve months in a year, and we take turns planning the date. When it is my turn, I try to find activities that I know will interest Randy. He does the same for me when his month rolls around. Your relationship with your husband should only be second to God on your priority list.

In the space below, list some ways that you can spend time with your husband. If you are single, list activities you can do with a friend at least once a month.

_____

_____

_____

_____

Here is an interesting thought: We work really hard to impress someone when we are dating. Then we work even harder to impress them in hopes that they will ask us to marry them. Then once we are married, we seem to fill our lives with so many other things that there is no time for the one we love. Why is that? We say we want to be married, but yet we live our married lives as if we were alone most of the time. When relationships become a priority, it is a sign along the way that you are learning to simplify your life.

Don't take your family and friends for granted. Enjoy every moment that you have together. Sometimes we don't realize what we have until it is gone. Savor the moment and make every effort to strengthen your relationships.

DAY 5
MAKING IT FUN

VERSE FOR THE DAY

I waited patiently for the Lord to help me, and he turned to me and heard my cry. He lifted me out of the pit of despair, out of the mud and the mire. He set my feet on solid ground and steadied me as I walked along. He has given me a new song to sing, a hymn of praise to our God. Many will see what he has done and be amazed. They will put their trust in the Lord.
Psalm 40:1-3 (NLT)

I encourage you to take some time today to count your blessings. So often we spend time in the pit of despair or as the Psalmist wrote, in the mud and the mire, and miss out on the gifts that God has given to us.

It is so easy to get caught up in self-pity when you look around and see clutter and past due bills. When you finally get a few minutes to watch the news or read the paper, all you get is bad news. I have heard it said that it takes ten "atta boys" to make up for one "got ya". In other words, you can have ten people compliment you on a new outfit and have one person tell you that they don't really think the color of your outfit goes with your complexion, and that is the only comment that you will remember.

Celebrate life today!

In the space below, list as many blessings as you have room to write.

Having trouble getting started? I'll help you.......

In spite of my mistakes, God still loves me! I have a roof over my head!

_____

_____

_____

_____

_____

_____

Did you notice that once you got started, the blessings just kept coming to mind? God is so good and loves you very much. He wants you to live a simpler life so that you can enjoy even more blessings!

I have discovered that the world really is full of good people. You just have to take time to notice. I have also discovered if I am nice to people, most people will be nice to me. As you go about your daily routine, make a mental note of the smiles, greetings, and acts of kindness others give to you. I hope you will be pleasantly surprised! Slow down enough to give others a smile, a friendly greeting, and an act of kindness.

Life is short so don't miss out on the good things – ask God to show you things worth celebrating today.

Did you list chocolate when you were writing down your blessings or things to celebrate? Remember that every good and perfect gift comes from God! As you celebrate life, take time to enjoy a piece of my favorite triple chocolate fudge cake, served warm with vanilla ice cream and chocolate syrup on top. To make it even more enjoyable, de-clutter your kitchen and invite some friends over. OR, put the kids to bed early, dim the lights, light some candles, and enjoy it with your husband. Who knows what might happen next?

HUMOR FOR THE DAY
Six-year-old Emily came home from school one day, and declared to her mother in a disgusted tone, "I never want to have kids. To get children you have to have sex!"

Her mother, shocked that her youngest of four children was even aware of the facts of life, let out an audible gasp.

Emily saw the shocked look on her mother's face and said, "What? You didn't know?"

THOUGHT FOR THE DAY
If you are not ready to take criticism, you are not prepared to succeed. Take inventory of your insecurities and promise yourself you will overcome them.

TODAY'S RECIPE

Triple Chocolate Fudge Cake

Prepare a 3 $\frac{1}{8}$ ounce package of chocolate pudding mix (cooked type) as directed on package. Blend chocolate cake mix (dry mix) into hot pudding. Pour ingredients into greased and floured 13 x 9 inch pan. Sprinkle with ½ cup semisweet chocolate pieces and ½ cup chopped nuts. Bake 30 to 35 minutes at 350 degrees.

PRAYER FOR THE DAY
Dear Heavenly Father,
Help me to focus my energy on good things today.
I want to celebrate life in you!
Thank you for blessing me with so much, and forgive me for the
times that I have been too busy to even notice.
Help me to simplify my life so that I may better serve you.
In your son's name, I pray.
Amen.

GROUP SESSION
WEEK 2

WHEN THE TIME IS RIGHT - GIVE IT AWAY

I. Imitate God, therefore, in everything you do, because _____ are his
    dear _____. Live a life filled with love, following the _____ of
    Christ. He _____ us and offered himself as a sacrifice for us, a pleasing
    _____ to God. Ephesians 5:1-2 (NLT)

II. _____- Give it away only when asked. When giving
     it away, you make room for more. Ask God to give you wisdom to know
     when to speak and when to lead by _____.

III. _____ - Whether we like it or not, we are
     creating_____ for those that we influence. When
     giving these away, you make room for more.

IV. _____- It's never too late to offer this through
    _____ _____, cards, kind words and smiles.
    When giving this away, you are making room for more opportunities.

V. To those who use well what they are _____, even more will be
    given, and they will have an abundance. But from those who do nothing,
    even what _____they have will be taken _____.
    Matthew 25:29 (NLT)

WEEK 3
A LIFE ANCHORED IN CONTENTMENT

April 2004 was an exciting month for me. I accomplished something that I dreamed of doing for years. With hard work, training, discipline, and encouragement from others, I completed the 26.2 mile Music City Marathon! Yes, you read that right, 26.2 miles! I had the option of running or walking, and I chose to walk. In order to receive the medal at the finish line, I was required to walk at a minimum pace of 15 minutes per mile. After many hours of walking, I could hear the crowd cheering and knew I was approaching the finish line. When it was in sight, my adrenaline kicked in, and I ran up the hill and across the finish line in time to receive my medal!

There were factors that had to be considered if I was to meet my goal. How badly did I want to do this? Was I committed enough to train for the event? In order to take on this challenge, what was I going to be giving up? What would people think? What if I couldn't do it? Was it worth my time?

I attended a meeting for the Leukemia Lymphoma Society, and they inspired me to train with them and to raise money for their organization. I had friends that had lost the battle with leukemia and had always wanted to do something in their memory. Once I signed up, I was determined to reach my goal. I trained 5 days a week on my own and every Saturday in the rain, sleet, snow, or hot sunshine with a team for six months. We started off with low mileage (5 miles) and worked our way up to 23 miles two weeks prior to the race. In order to take on this challenge, I had to give up my warm bed very early on Saturday mornings. As we got closer to race day, the time spent training lasted longer. Not to mention that I also had to rest and recover for at least an hour and a half when I got home. My husband was very supportive, but I'm sure he thought I was crazy when the temperature was in the low teens and I would crawl out of bed, put on layers of clothes and head out the door on Saturdays. My children just nodded their heads as if to say, "I'm so not interested in this, but I'll humor Mom by acting like I am anyway." My co-workers and friends just thought I was crazy, and I don't think they really thought I could accomplish my goal. In the back of my mind, I was fearful that I would not be able to reach the finish line. I knew others that were older than me had done it, but I still had that thread of doubt that would creep in and cause me to want to give up for fear of failure.

DAY 1
One Day at a Time

DAY 2
Loving Your Life Enough to Protect It

DAY 3
Hide and Seek

DAY 4
Find and Keep

DAY 5
Making it Fun

The things that kept me going were simple things, but without them, I never could have reached my goal. My faith in God, my encouraging team in training, a friend that believed in me, a child with leukemia that was counting on me. Was it worth it? Absolutely! I raised $2500.00 for the Leukemia Lymphoma Society, I inspired others to train for the upcoming race, I met a wonderful group of women, and best of all, I proved to myself that if I focus on my goals, I can cross the finish line and get the medal to prove it!

In this third unit of study, we will begin to map out a plan for a simpler life. We will look at ways to manage time better. Some people might call this the Time Management Unit. Without a plan, life will remain chaotic for you and your family. It will require some training and hard work, but the end result can be very rewarding.

Nothing worth having comes easy!

Anticipate all God wants to teach you this week! Ask Him to show you the things that He wants you to see everyday as you study His word. Be open to a fresh and new approach to life!

DAY 1
ONE DAY AT A TIME

VERSES FOR THE DAY

"So don't worry about tomorrow, for tomorrow will bring its own worries. Today's trouble is enough for today."
Matthew 6:34 (NLT)

Commit everything you do to the Lord. Trust him, and he will help you.
Psalm 37:5 (NLT)

Live wisely among those who are not believers, and make the most of every opportunity.
Colossians 4:5 (NLT)

I don't mean to say that I have already achieved these things or that I have already reached perfection. But I press on to possess that perfection for which Christ Jesus first possessed me. No, dear brothers and sisters, I have not achieved it, but I focus on this one thing: Forgetting the past and looking forward to what lies ahead, I press on to reach the end of the race and receive the heavenly prize for which God, through Christ Jesus, is calling us.
Philippians 3:12-14 (NLT)

When you start feeling that your life is getting under control or that a simpler lifestyle can actually be a reality, do you find that "life" gets in the way and everything falls apart? Do you look at the "stuff" around you and convince yourself that the only way out of the mess is to sell the house "as is", stuff and all, and start over?

Before going any further in the lesson today, close your eyes, take three deep breaths, count to 50 (slowly) and then write a prayer asking God to comfort your soul and rest your racing mind.

_____

_____

_____

_____

Recently, I was working on a project at work that involved heavy negotiations. I was part of a negotiation team that consisted of a real estate broker, an accountant, and two attorneys. During the course of the negotiations, the accountant, who happens to be a co-worker, was to be out of town for a few days and could not be reached. His instructions for me before leaving town were, "Don't blow it." I know he was joking with me (I think), but at the same time, it caused me to think about the situation in a different light. I had every intention of handling things in the most professional way possible, and I knew that I could not finalize the deal quickly. There were still many aspects of the negotiating that had to be done before it was complete. In an effort to keep things running smoothly during his absence, I knew I needed to devise a plan and do my best to make sure nothing fell through the cracks. In other words, I wanted to make sure that I didn't blow it. Just so you know the rest of the story, I am pleased to announce that everything went smoothly, even in his absence, and all negotiations are now final. AND...I didn't blow it!

There were times during the negotiations when we thought all parties were going to agree. Then something unexpected would happen, and we would have to start back at square one. I have learned that any time you have more than one person working on a project, there is bound to be conflict. We had a goal in mind, and that goal was to finalize the negotiations, create a contract that all parties could agree upon, and receive the proper signatures for execution. After six months of negotiating, it finally happened. We now have a done deal!

What if I had blown it? What if I had allowed "stuff" to get in the way? What if I had given up halfway through the project? I would never have experienced the satisfaction of completing the task and reaching the goal.

Your life's goals are very similar to this in that when you set your sights on the goal before you and begin to focus on the plan of action, "stuff" or "life" will get in the way. It can be very tempting to get discouraged and just give up. Let's look at some things you can do to avoid setbacks.

In the space below, write your long- range goal:

_____

_____

_____

In the space below, write some short-term goals:

_____

_____

_____

It is great that you are beginning to focus on your goals, and in order to accomplish them, I suggest that you take one day at a time. Let's do an assessment of your situation right now.

HUMOR FOR THE DAY

Did you hear about the doctor who went on a ski trip and got lost on the slopes? He stamped out "help" in the snow, but nobody could read his writing.

Place a check by the statement(s) that applies to you.

____ I know I need to make some changes and I'm thinking about how to get started.

____ I have written my goals down, now I need to formulate a plan.

____ I realize that "stuff" or "life' will interrupt my plan, but I will not allow this to get me down.

____ I need to be patient with myself and take one step at a time.

You didn't get into the shape you are in overnight, so don't expect to get out of it overnight.

It is good to have long-range goals. I encourage you to dream big dreams with expectations that they will come true. If you are striving for perfection and expecting a quick fix, I am afraid you are setting yourself up for failure. I would like to suggest that you take one day at a time. A baby has to crawl before it can walk. In the same way, you will be motivated to keep working on the areas that are out of control if you start small and work your way up to completion. Notice I did not write "work your way up to perfection." Most people that strive for perfection are prone to procrastination. Most of the time when they discover that life is out of control, their mindset is that in order to correct the situation, they will need a full day or a full week to make everything perfect again, so they "wait" until there is time to do it right. Guess what happens? Nothing! Why? Because there is never enough time to make things perfect. Let's strive for improvement instead.

When I was a little girl, my mother had a set schedule for every day. It was a good schedule, and everyone in the family knew what chores were to be done on any given day. I remember that Monday was Laundry Day. She kept the household organized, and the meals were also planned ahead of time. There were certain things that were set in stone at our house, and only an emergency could change the plan. I learned at a very young age what was important to my parents and to this day, will not waiver from their teachings. Thanks, Mom!

My parents taught me to live a simple life with good values. Every morning, my parents took time to gather around the breakfast table to read God's word and pray with me. This taught me that starting the day with God's blessings was important to my parents and therefore should be important to me. Even though I worked full time when my children were growing up, I continued the tradition with them in my household. I pray that they will do the same for their children. What can you do to teach your children the importance of living a simpler life?

Be careful! Your schedule can get filled before you even have time to plan for it. Look over the list below and mark the things that need to be done on a regular basis. Put a D for daily, W for weekly and M for monthly:

___Pay Bills	___Bible Study	___Laundry
___Balance Checkbook	___Exercise	___Prepare Meals
___Children's Activities	___Help with Homework	___Clean Bathrooms
___Yard Work	___Grocery Shopping	___Change Bed Linens
___Wash Dishes	___Dust & Vacuum	___Shop for Clothes

Any of the items listed above that need to be done on a weekly basis could be assigned a certain day of the week. Instead of trying to do everything on Saturday, designate other days during the week to get things done. One of my goals has been to make Saturday my "play day." This goal is attainable IF I take care of the chores during the week. Then everything is caught up before the weekend. This doesn't always happen, but when it does, I have fun shopping, reading, going somewhere with my husband or playing with children.

Below, write mini goals for each day that will enable you to reach bigger ones in the future.

MONDAY_____

_____

TUESDAY _____

_____

WEDNESDAY_____

_____

THURSDAY _____

_____

FRIDAY _____

_____

SATURDAY _____

_____

SUNDAY _____

_____

The above exercise is a test. You might not get all of the answers right this week. Try sticking with your plan throughout the week and then make the necessary changes for improvement before next week. I love having Saturdays free to attend Women's Retreats, sleep late, spend time with friends, watch a ballgame, or rest. You can do this too. You simply have to plan for it.

Ten Simple Home Rules For Everyone to Live By:

1. If you sleep on it...make it up.
2. If you wear it...hang it up.
3. If you drop it...pick it up.
4. If you eat out of it...put it in the sink.
5. If you step on it...wipe it off.
6. If you open it...close it.
7. If you empty it...fill it up.
8. If it rings...answer it.
9. If it howls...feed it.
10. If it cries...love it.

SHINEWORTHY TEA

5348 Hickory Hollow Pkwy
Antioch, Tennessee
37013

SHINEWORTHY TEA

TOTAL
$16.39

Item	Price
SIMPLIFY	**$15.00**
SUBTOTAL	**$15.00**
Davidson County Tax (2.25%)	**$0.34**
TN State Tax (7%)	**$1.05**
TOTAL	**$16.39**
CASH	**$20.00**
CHANGE DUE	**$3.61**

Date: January 16, 2015, 9:54 AM
Sold by: Sue Ann C
Order: #1-1951

Thank You!

DAY 2

LOVING YOUR LIFE ENOUGH
TO PROTECT IT

VERSES FOR THE DAY

And so, dear brothers and sisters, I plead with you to give your bodies to God because of all he has done for you. Let them be a living and holy sacrifice—the kind he will find acceptable. This is truly the way to worship him. Romans 12:1 (NLT)

Everyone must submit to governing authorities. For all authority comes from God, and those in positions of authority have been placed there by God. So anyone who rebels against authority is rebelling against what God has instituted, and they will be punished. For the authorities do not strike fear in people who are doing right, but in those who are doing wrong. Would you like to live without fear of the authorities? Do what is right, and they will honor you. The authorities are God's servants, sent for your good. But if you are doing wrong, of course you should be afraid, for they have the power to punish you. They are God's servants, sent for the very purpose of punishing those who do what is wrong. So you must submit to them, not only to avoid punishment, but also to keep a clear conscience. Romans 13:1–5 (NLT)

Owe nothing to anyone—except for your obligation to love one another. If you love your neighbor, you will fulfill the requirements of God's law. Romans 13:8 (NLT)

Run from sexual sin! No other sin so clearly affects the body as this one does. For sexual immorality is a sin against your own body. Don't you realize that your body is the temple of the Holy Spirit, who lives in you and was given to you by God? You do not belong to yourself. I Corinthians 6:18–19 (NLT)

Don't you realize that in a race everyone runs, but only one person gets the prize? So run to win! All athletes are disciplined in their training. They do it to win a prize that will fade away, but we do it for an eternal prize. So I run with purpose in every step. I am not just shadowboxing. I discipline my body like an athlete, training it to do what it should. Otherwise, I fear that after preaching to others I myself might be disqualified. I Corinthians 9:24–27 (NLT)

Don't act thoughtlessly, but understand what the Lord wants you to do. Don't be drunk with wine, because that will ruin your life. Instead, be filled with the Holy Spirit. Ephesians 5:17–18 (NLT)

In Psalm 40, the Psalmist writes, "He lifted me out of the pit of despair, out of the mud and the mire." How does one end up in the mud and the mire? I strongly believe that the choices we make determine the outcome of our lives. Sometimes the wrong choices are done innocently at first and then become a habit of life.

If you are sincere in wanting to live a simplified life, then you must be willing to protect yourself from things that can cause harm to your body, mind, and soul! You must love your life enough to protect it! You are not only protecting your life from your own foolish choices, but the influence of others and Satan's schemes.

Beginning each day with a Bible study and prayer is an essential key to success in this area. When you ask God to show you the things that He wants you to see and are willing to pay attention, He will show you the areas of your life that are not right with Him. Write a prayer below asking him to show you the areas of your life that need protection.

_____

_____

_____

One area that most women struggle in is self-esteem. Feelings of worthlessness, doubt and depression can take over if you spend most of your time listening to the worldviews around you. You begin to condemn yourself for being overweight, or having debt, or for a lack of will power when out with friends. The next thing you know, you start thinking that you cannot possibly be around your church friends because you are a disgrace to all that they stand for. How did this happen? When did this happen? Is there a way out? Well, I'm here to tell you that there most certainly is a way out. The first thing that must be done is for you to get on your knees and repent of your sins to God, your Heavenly Father. Then you must accept His forgiveness and begin to look at your life as the precious gift from God that it is. God sent His only son to die on a cruel cross in order for you to have salvation and an abundant life.

Write the words from John 3:16 in the space below.

_____

_____

_____

God wants only the best for you and I pray that you will feel the same way about yourself that God does. In Psalm 139:13 – 17 it says that He made all the delicate, inner parts of your body and knit YOU together in your mother's womb. Thank God for making you so wonderfully complex! His workmanship is marvelous. He watched YOU as YOU were being formed in utter seclusion, as YOU were woven together in the dark of the womb. He saw YOU before YOU were born. Every moment was laid out before a single day had passed. How precious are His thoughts about YOU! They are innumerable!

God loves you more than words could ever describe. Because of His great love for you, I encourage you to love your life enough to protect it!

In the space below, list things that you seek protection from:

_____

_____

_____

THOUGHT FOR THE DAY
Self-doubt has been the ruin of many dream seekers. Confidence has given rise to those who have succeeded. Believe in yourself and win!

If you are hanging out with the "wrong" crowd (anyone that tries to bring you down or encourages you to do things that are in direct opposition of God's teachings in your life) then pray like the Psalmist in Psalm 140:1–3; O Lord, rescue me from evil people. Protect me from those who are violent, those who plot evil in their hearts and stir up trouble all day long. Their tongues sting like a snake; the venom of a viper drips from their lips.

Step 1 in protecting your life is to <u>choose your friends wisely</u>. A true friend will not try to get you to do anything that is against God's teaching. A true friend will hold you accountable for the wrong choices that you make.

Take control of what I say, O Lord, and guard my lips. Don't let me drift toward evil or take part in acts of wickedness. Don't let me share in the delicacies of those who do wrong. Psalm 141:3-4 (NLT)

Step 2 in protecting your life is to <u>do your best to live at peace with everyone</u>. In Romans 12:18, it says, "Do all that you can to live in peace with everyone." Your life will be protected from heartache and pain if you will treat others with the utmost dignity and respect. If you have a hard time doing this, ask God to help you understand why people treat you the way that they do or why they act like they do. I have found that remaining calm and holding my tongue allows me to keep my relationships in check, and I avoid feeling hurt by others. I have also learned that I cannot take things personally when someone comes across angry or mad at me. Sometimes the other person is simply having a bad

PRAYER FOR THE DAY
Dear Heavenly
Father,
Thank you for
the reminders in
your word of your
great love for me.
Protect me from
evil and guide my
footsteps.
May I live this
day in a way that
pleases you.
Help me to make
choices that will
enable me to live
a simple life, a
life that longs to
know you more
and serve you
daily.
In your son's
name, I pray.
Amen.

day, and I just happened to be in their line of fire at the least opportune time.

Step 3 in protecting your life is to <u>pay your debts on time.</u> I encourage you to take this a step further and eliminate your debt as quickly as possible. If you are behind on your payments, then you will continually be in a bad mood or will avoid answering the phone for fear of the intimidation of the "collector."

Step 4 in protecting your life is to <u>stay away from sinful lifestyles.</u> Nothing good will come out of a sinful lifestyle. You will find yourself running away from anyone or anything that exposes the sin in your life. One of the first things that most people do when they begin to live in opposition to God's word is run away from God. I have discovered that God has a way of getting your attention when you run away from Him. It is better to confess your sins and repent of your evil ways before God's wrath comes upon you!

Step 5 in protecting your life is to <u>take your physical well-being seriously.</u> There are many good benefits to eating healthy and exercising daily. Take a look at the list below for some of the reasons exercise has been proven to enrich the quality of your life:

1. Increases your self-esteem
2. Improves your digestion
3. Gives you more energy
4. Helps you sleep better
5. Adds a sparkle and radiance to your complexion
6. Improves your body shape

I have a list of over 100 ways exercise will enrich the quality of your life. Due to the space restraints, I could only list the first six. If you would like the complete list, feel free to email me at **sueann@shineworthy.com**. Be sure and schedule your annual checkups with your Gynecologist and your Primary Care Physician. It is equally important to see your dentist twice a year for a cleaning and check up. **Early detection in most cases can save your life!**

Step 6 in protecting your life is to <u>practice self discipline in areas such as sex, alcohol, finances, and relationships.</u> Being a Christian does not mean you have to join a convent in order to be pleasing to God. It does mean that you are to conduct yourself in a manner pleasing to Him in all areas. Years ago the following question began to appear on t-shirts, bracelets, billboards, and as book titles. WHAT WOULD JESUS DO? This is a very good question to ask yourself when you are tempted to step over the line. God's word is the best resource you have for protecting yourself against sin, hurts and bad choices.

Don't let evil conquer you, but conquer evil by doing good. Romans 12:21 (NLT)

As you strive to live a simpler life, take time today to identify choices that you are making that are complicating your life. Ask God to help you get back on track and protect you from your own evil desires and wrong choices.

_____

_____

_____

Pay careful attention to your own work, for then you will get the satisfaction of a job well done, and you won't need to compare yourself to anyone else. For we are each responsible for our own conduct. Galatians 6:4-5 (NLT)

DAY 3
HIDE AND SEEK

VERSES FOR THE DAY

"If a man has a hundred sheep and one of them wanders away, what will he do? Won't he leave the ninety-nine others on the hills and go out to search for the one that is lost? And if he finds it, I tell you the truth, he will rejoice over it more than over the ninety-nine that didn't wander away! In the same way, it is not my heavenly Father's will that even one of these little ones should perish."
Matthew 18:12-14 (NLT)

"Or suppose a woman has ten silver coins and loses one. Won't she light a lamp and sweep the entire house and search carefully until she finds it? And when she finds it, she will call in her friends and neighbors and say, 'Rejoice with me because I have found my lost coin.' In the same way, there is joy in the presence of God's angels when even one sinner repents."
Luke 15:8 -10 (NLT)

Pay careful attention to your own work, for then you will get the satisfaction of a job well done, and you won't need to compare yourself to anyone else. For we are each responsible for our own conduct.
Galatians 6:4-5 (NLT)

If I had a nickel for all the times that I have spent looking for an important item at the last minute, I would probably be a millionaire by now! There have been times when I have been rushing to get to a meeting or to work only to discover my car keys were missing. I have a bad habit of taking off my shoes when I come home and leaving them in different rooms in the house. When I decide to wear them again, I can never remember where I last put them. Oh, and then there are those important papers that I put in a "special place" so that I can find them the next time I need them. You guessed it...I don't remember where I put them when I need them again. Does this ever happen to you? I have come home from the grocery store, put my groceries away and gone back into the kitchen later to prepare a meal and forgotten where I put the very items needed for that meal. Have you ever lost your car?

Just for giggles and grins, list some of the things that you have lost or seem to lose on a regular basis.

_____

_____

_____

I've tried to come up with different excuses as to why I lose things. Sometimes I blame the neighbors of coming over in the middle of the night and hiding things from me just so they can watch me panic through the window the next morning. (Not really. I am being sarcastic.) There are times when you really can blame the toddler in the house for missing shoes, keys, grocery items, and your missing purse. I know people that have been stranded because their toddler was playing with their car keys and when asked where they put them, they couldn't remember. So for many hours they were in an all out search only to find that the toddler had thrown them into the toilet. So if this ever happens to you, one of the first places you might want to look is in the bathroom!

In order to plan ahead, do you sometimes buy gifts in advance? If you happen to find something on sale and have the money to purchase it, then you have taken a step in the right direction toward managing your time and money better. But, when it is time to wrap the gift and give it away, do you remember where you put it?

It is a good idea to create a shopping list before going to the store. This saves time and keeps you from making multiple trips back to the store to purchase items you forgot the first time. But, how many times do you lose the list or forget to take it with you?

Have you ever left your child at church or school because you forgot to pick them up? OR were so busy taking care of your obligations that you left in a hurry and realized later (when someone called) that they weren't in the car with you?

Do your children lose their homework, books, or important papers? Whose footsteps are they following?

PLAYING HIDE AND SEEK IS A MAJOR TIME WASTER!

Think of all the time wasted searching for lost items. Imagine what it could be like if you didn't have to spend so much time and energy looking under beds, behind doors, in toy boxes, or digging through the piles of clutter to find things. If you are doing this most every day, I venture to say that you stay pretty stressed out most of the time.

SLOW DOWN! If you are always on the go and never taking time to rest, plan, and pray, then you will continue wasting time in search of lost items. When your mind is racing all the time, it can be difficult to remember the simplest things. Things such as why you got up from the sofa and went into the kitchen. Have you ever had to retrace your steps and talk to yourself about why you needed to go from one place to another? This is a sure sign that you are way too busy!

**PRAYER FOR
THE DAY**

Dear Heavenly
Father,
Help me to slow
down and focus
on the things in
life that you want
me to see.
Give me guidance
and wisdom as I
examine areas of
my life that need
improvement.
Teach me your
ways.
In your son's
name, I pray.
Amen.

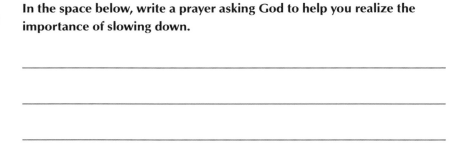

In the space below, write a prayer asking God to help you realize the importance of slowing down.

_____

_____

_____

GET ORGANIZED!

Deep down inside, I believe every woman wants to feel she is organized. If you are losing things on a regular basis, then Girlfriend, you have some work to do!

Circle the items below that seem to be missing most anytime that you need them:

Phone Book	Pen	Notepad	Coupons
Water Bill	Checkbook	Tape	Recipes
Bible	Address Book	Wrapping Paper	Scissors
Jewelry	Hair Bows	Tape Measure	

In the space below, identify specific items that need to have designated areas in your home.

_____

_____

_____

Once you have identified items that need to have designated areas, then the next step is to decide where you will place these items. Then when you use the item, simply place it back in the designated area. The next time you need it, you will be able to find it! Sounds simple, but it will take some practice. Think of all the time, energy and stress you can save by keeping things organized. If you have toddlers in the house, I would suggest that most designated areas be high enough that they cannot reach them.

DAY 4

FIND AND KEEP

I heard an advertisement on the radio this week about an event that was to take place on a showboat. The announcer said, "Get your tickets now for a nice restful and relaxing dinner on the **hurricane deck** of the General Jackson." When I think of hurricanes, I don't usually equate them with restful and relaxing times. Do you? As I began to think about this, I realized that it really is possible to have peace and contentment in the midst of a storm or hurricane.

Have you ever been around someone that is battling a terminal disease? Once they accept the news of their condition, they will have a peace that comes over them that is unexplainable in human terms. The secret ingredient is a right relationship with God.

As you strive to simplify your life, remember that it will take some time to get things back under control. But in the meantime, learn to be content in knowing that in the midst of the storm, you can have peace. Peace in knowing that there really is a light at the end of the tunnel. Peace in knowing that you have a promise that if you practice all that you have learned from God's word, He will be with you. In Luke 8:22-25, we read about a time when the apostles

VERSES FOR THE DAY

Don't love money; be satisfied with what you have. For God has said, "I will never fail you. I will never abandon you." So we can say with confidence, "The Lord is my helper, so I will have no fear. What can mere people do to me?" Hebrews 13:5-6 (NLT)

Keep putting into practice all you learned and received from me—everything you heard from me and saw me doing. Then the God of peace will be with you. Philippians 4:9 (NLT)

One day Jesus said to his disciples, "Let's cross to the other side of the lake." So they got into a boat and started out. As they sailed across, Jesus settled down for a nap. But soon a fierce storm came down on the lake. The boat was filling with water, and they were in real danger. The disciples went and woke him up, shouting, "Master, Master, we're going to drown!" When Jesus woke up, he rebuked the wind and the raging waves. Suddenly the storm stopped and all was calm. Then he asked them, "Where is your faith?" The disciples were terrified and amazed. "Who is this man?" they asked each other. "When he gives a command, even the wind and waves obey him!" Luke 8:22-25 (NLT)

A mother was preparing pancakes for her sons, Kevin, 5 and Ryan, 3. The boys began to argue over who would get the first pancake. Their mother saw the opportunity for a moral lesson. If Jesus were sitting here, He would say, "Let my brother have the first pancake, I can wait." Kevin turned to his younger brother and said, "Ryan, you be Jesus."

were out on the seas when a storm came up that frightened them very much. In the middle of the storm, Jesus remained rested and relaxed. They felt that he needed to be awakened during the storm and could not understand how he could remain so calm. The Bible says that He rebuked the wind and the raging waves. The storm stopped, and all was calm once again.

As you examine your life, how can you find peace and contentment even before everything is back under control? The answer is through God and his word. When you look around your house or any part of your life that seems out of control, remind yourself that you can experience peace if you seek to find it.

One way to find peace and keep it is through God's word.

I have hidden your word in my heart, that I might not sin against you.
Psalm 119:11 (NLT)

How do you hide God's word in your heart? _____

There are times when I feel scared or frustrated in a situation and a verse of scripture will come to mind. In remembering the scriptures, I can diffuse a difficult situation.

In the space below, write a verse from God's word that you will memorize today.

_____

_____

_____

Another way to find peace and keep it is through prayer.

Don't worry about anything; instead, pray about everything. Tell God what you need, and thank him for all he has done. Then you will experience God's peace, which exceeds anything we can understand. His peace will guard your hearts and minds as you live in Christ Jesus.
Philippians 4:6-7 (NLT)

In the space below, write a prayer to God asking him to help you strengthen your prayer life.

_____

_____

_____

THOUGHT FOR THE DAY
Allow people to invest personally in your dream by praying for you on a regular basis.

The third way that you can find peace and keep it is through determination.

Be determined not to stray from your plan, and keep working toward the goal of a simpler lifestyle.

When something or someone gets in the way of your well thought out plan, don't take a turn in the wrong direction. Stay determined to keep your eyes focused on the goal. When you are making strides toward a simpler life, lots of interruptions will come into play. Be like the Energizer Bunny, and just keep on going. Don't stop!

In the space below, list times when finding peace can be difficult.

_____

_____

_____

Finders should be keepers when it comes to peace and contentment. Satan would like nothing better than to keep your life so busy and full of chaos that you make no time to find peace, much less keep it. When you are feeling overwhelmed, remember God is ultimately in control of the situation and rest in His blessed assurance and peace!

Take a serious look at the list and apply the three principles to each situation and see if contentment and peace overtake the feelings of frustration, stress, and frenzy.

Ask yourself the following questions:

1. Is there an answer to my dilemma in the Bible?

2. Will God listen when I pray?

3. Will determination allow me to take back control?

The answer to all three questions should be "yes." I challenge you to examine your situation and find peace in the midst of your storm. Find a restful and relaxing dinner on the Hurricane Deck!

DAY 5

MAKING IT FUN

Don't forget to incorporate some fun activities into this day. I like to declare Fridays as "Fun-filled Fridays." I used to have an assistant that would get aggravated at me when I would come in to the office on Fridays and say, "Okay, lets make every effort to make this a fun-filled Friday." She would stomp her foot and with big tears in her eyes, she would say, "Sue Ann, you say that every week, and I don't ever have a fun-filled Friday."

Now that I think about it, I don't think she ever had a fun-filled anything! How do you view life? Is the glass half full or half empty? Do you look for the good in a situation or just expect the worst?

Let's think of ways to make this a fun-filled day!

VERSES FOR THE DAY

Imitate God, therefore, in everything you do, because you are his dear children.
Ephesians 5:1 (NLT)

Let all that I am wait quietly before God, for my hope is in him. He alone is my rock and my salvation, my fortress where I will not be shaken.
Psalm 62:5-6 (NLT)

Choose a good reputation over great riches; being held in high esteem is better than silver or gold. The rich and poor have this in common: The Lord made them both.
Proverbs 22:1-2 (NLT)

Direct your children onto the right path, and when they are older, they will not leave it.
Proverbs 22:6 (NLT)

A wife invited some people to dinner. At the table, she turned to her six-year-old daughter and said, "Would you like to say the blessing?"

"I wouldn't know what to say," the girl replied.

"Just say what you hear Mommy say," the wife answered.

The daughter bowed her head and said, "Lord, why on earth did I invite all of these people to dinner?"

Start the day off by thanking God for the gift of another day.

_____

_____

_____

In the space below, write a prayer to God asking him to show you reasons to laugh and have fun today.

_____

_____

_____

List an area that you will de-clutter today:

_____

_____

_____

If time permits, go to the Mall and watch the people. Say a prayer for each person that passes by. This is a great way to be reminded of God's love for everyone.

Write a press release to an imaginary newspaper. Tell all about your journey to success and be sure to list the names of people who've helped you along the way. (Don't forget the famous and infamous.) Tuck this away in a safe place and read it when you feel discouraged.

_____

_____

_____

Focus on five things that make you happy to be who you are.

1. _____

2. _____

3. _____

4. _____

5. _____

In the space below, write down something that made you laugh or smile today.

_____

_____

_____

While you put the finishing touches on a de-clutter project or finish folding the laundry, consider placing the following dessert in the oven. This is one of my husband's favorite recipes. It is especially delicious with vanilla ice cream and topped with caramel sauce.

TODAY'S RECIPE

APPLE DELIGHT

Take two cans of apple pie filling and place it in the bottom of a 9x12 inch dish. Top with dry butter pecan cake mix. Finish it off with two sticks of margarine that are cut into small pieces to cover the top. Place in oven and bake at 350 degrees for 30 minutes.
Enjoy!

Your house will smell soooo good while this dessert is baking. Time it where you can place it in the oven just before your husband or children come home. The aroma will fill your house with love!

GROUP SESSION

MOVE OUT THE CLOUDS AND MAKE ROOM FOR SUNLIGHT

God wants to _____you and give you his _____.

How _____ is the goodness you have stored up for those who _____ you. You lavish it on those who come to you for _____, _____ them before the watching _____. Psalm 31:19

I.   Even when your situation seems _____, _____, or _____, don't give up without even trying!

Let your favor _____on your servant. In your _____ love, rescue me. Psalm 31:16

II. Remember that God is _____ with _____!

Once I was young, and now I am _____. Yet I have never seen the godly abandoned, or their children begging for _____. Psalm 37:25

How do you see the world? How do you see the circumstances around you? Do you look at life through rose colored glasses or are you an active member of the Doom and Gloom Club? Do you feel defeated before the battle even begins?

With God's help, you can conquer every fear, see things through His eyes, and resign from the Doom and Gloom Club! He will go with you right into the fog and bring you into the bright sunshine!

For I can do _____through Christ, who gives me _____. Philippians 4:13

WEEK 4
A LIFE ANCHORED IN JOY

Making a "To Do List" is a good step to take when trying to simplify your life. However, when you take time to write down all the many things that need to be done, it can be overwhelming. It's like dreaming the impossible dream to actually think you might be able to accomplish everything on the list in one day. I don't know about you, but most days I end up moving unfinished items to the next day's list only to find that there is no time on that day to complete the tasks either. After a few days, some of the tasks are removed from the list and placed on a "pending" list. Most of the time the pending list is tucked out of sight and just as the old saying goes, "Out of sight, out of mind." I never seem to get around to those items again.

In this fourth unit of study, we will look at ways to improve in areas that seem to clutter and cloud our minds in such a way that life seems more complicated than it should. How many times have you said, "I meant to do that but just never got around to it"?

Anticipate all God wants to teach you this week! Ask Him to show you the things He wants you to see everyday as you study His word. Be open to a fresh and new approach to life!

DAY 1
Lost in
the Sea of
Forgetfulness

DAY 2
Walking the
Tight Wire

DAY 3
Two Basic
Principles of
Life

DAY 4
Smoke and
Mirrors

DAY 5
Making it Fun

DAY 1

LOST IN THE SEA OF FORGETFULNESS

With the busy schedules that most women keep, it has become harder and harder to keep up with the needs of others and to take the time to offer encouragement in their struggles. I don't like admitting this, but I have purchased gifts and cards for friends that were going through difficult struggles and never delivered or mailed them.

My intentions were good, but for some reason, my follow through was lousy.

How many times have you received invitations to showers, birthday parties, Pampered Chef parties, Tupperware parties, weddings, committee meetings, or other special events and realized after the fact that you simply forgot to RSVP or even worse, forgot to attend? When this happens, it's time to re-evaluate the situation and get organized once again.

Daily planners are great tools if used properly. It is a good idea to carry your planner with you everywhere you go. When you are waiting at a traffic light or in a car pool line, pull out the planner and review the upcoming activities. In order for this system to work properly, two things have to occur. First, you need to write the event in your planner. Next, you will need to refer to it throughout your day.

In looking over your calendar everyday, make note of gifts and cards that you need to purchase, as well as phone calls and visits you might need to work into your schedule. If you get into a habit of checking things out ahead of time, you will avoid last minute trips to the store, and last minute costly expenditures.

VERSES FOR THE DAY

If you are wise and understand God's ways, prove it by living an honorable life, doing good works with the humility that comes from wisdom.
James 3:13 (NLT)

Indeed, we all make many mistakes. For if we could control our tongues, we would be perfect and could also control ourselves in every other way.
James 3:2 (NLT)

Live wisely among those who are not believers, and make the most of every opportunity. Let your conversation be gracious and attractive so that you will have the right response for everyone.
Colossians 4:5-6 (NLT)

Here is my advice: It would be good for you to finish what you started a year ago. Last year you were the first who wanted to give, and you were the first to begin doing it. Now you should finish what you started. Let the eagerness you showed in the beginning be matched now by your giving. Give in proportion to what you have.
2 Corinthians 8:10-11 (NLT)

Just think how much more enjoyable special events will be if you simply plan ahead!

When I was living at home with my parents, a family in the church invited us to dinner. We arrived on time, and the hostess seemed somewhat irritated that we showed up "unannounced" right at their dinner hour. My parents thought this seemed somewhat strange but realized early on that the hostess had obviously forgotten she had invited us for dinner. We visited with the family for about thirty minutes and then left. It wasn't until later in the week that the woman realized why we showed up right at the dinner hour. Needless to say, she was very embarrassed. So embarrassed that she made up for it at a later date with a spectacular spread of food. Probably more than she would have originally done. I am thankful that this has not happened to me, but I can understand how easy this could happen to any of us.

I'm convinced that we have really good intentions, but life gets in the way, and we simply forget to follow through. In the space below, list some times when you have had good intentions and simply forgot to follow through.

_____

_____

_____

Today, I want to offer some reasons to avoid falling into the sea of forgetfulness.

Parties and Special Events:
If you forget about the event, you will miss out on the fun. Girlfriends need to have fun! When you are invited to something, write it down. Write it in your planner, on your wall calendar, and on your desk calendar. If necessary, send yourself a reminder e-mail!

Opportunities to Encourage Others:
Do you remember the last time you were ill or had a tragedy in your family? How did you feel when you received cards, phone calls, or flowers? Even if the person appears to have it all together, your message of encouragement could be exactly what they need that day. Don't assume you have nothing to offer. When you realize the impact that your act of encouragement will have on others, it will be easier to remember to follow through and actually mail the card!

Opportunities to Support Others:

Sometimes I wonder if women really understand what it says to someone when you simply forget to come to their event. Even if you don't feel this way, it says to the hostess and others that attended that you are too busy to spend time with them. If you take time to show up, it says just the opposite. It says that you are supporting their endeavors and what they do matters to you.

Opportunities to Build Trust:

If you tell someone you are going to show up or that you will take care of something and you forget to do it, then they will begin to think you cannot be trusted. They will doubt your sincerity and lose confidence in your abilities to follow through. It is important to do what you say you will do. Do what ever it takes to remember to take care of the thing you said you would do. *Write it down, and keep the list in a convenient place as a reminder.*

So much stress and an unorganized lifestyle reverts back to the fact that you did not take time to follow through. When this is realized, it causes tension among friends, coworkers, and family members. Not to mention what it does to your guilt complex!

Keep a planner or note pad with you at all times and refer to it throughout the day. A major component in a simpler life is to follow through on good intentions. Some would say it like this, " *Don't just talk the talk...take time to walk the walk!"*

Don't underestimate the impression you have on others. Your encouragement, support, and trust should not be taken lightly. If someone takes time to invite you to an event or tells you about a struggle or tragedy in their life, it is because they need you. *Clean out the clutter in your life and make room for others!*

I find that the best time for me to write cards of encouragement, or to look over my calendar is first thing in the morning during my prayer time. I ask God to give me names of people that might need an extra dose of encouragement and support. I also check to see if there are any conflicts on my calendar. If I rely on my own strength in this area, I will continue to swim around in the sea of forgetfulness. I ask God to help me in this area daily, and He has been faithful every time!

PRAYER FOR THE DAY

Dear Heavenly Father,
I ask that you will guide me as I take steps toward a simpler life. Help me to remember the things that need to be done in my life and for others. Show me how to be an encourager to others and to keep my word. In your son's name, I pray. Amen.

In the space below, write a prayer to God asking Him to show you the areas of follow through that you need to improve upon and to give you the guidance needed to make the necessary changes.

_____

_____

_____

Find a designated area in your house for all occasion cards, stamps, envelopes, and a pen so that you will have everything you need available when you need to brighten someone's day.

DAY 2

WALKING THE TIGHT WIRE

When my son was a senior in high school, I realized he had never been to "The Greatest Show on Earth", Barnum and Bailey's Circus. So at the age of seventeen, he and I traveled to a nearby city to take in the experience of elephants, tigers, and bears! We saw men and women on the flying trapeze, clowns being shot out of canons, and poodles doing amazing tricks. One of the most amazing feats of all was watching men and women walk across the tight wire. At first they walked one after another, then they walked across with someone on their shoulders. And if that wasn't scary enough, they walked across with two people on their shoulders. In order to stay balanced, they held a pole that had equal weight on both ends, and they remained very focused. The wire that they walked across was at least thirty feet in the air with a safety net below in case they slipped and fell. I'm not sure which one of us enjoyed the experience more, my son or me!

It can be difficult to juggle everything in our daily lives and find balance in all the different areas.

I think most women really want to simplify and find balance in life, but confusion can set in if you get your advice from the wrong sources. When you are standing in line at the grocery store, it seems that one can be bombarded with magazines full of advice for living a better life. They offer ways to have better sex, stronger abs, perfect children, guilt-free diets, better homes, perfect skin, great hair, and on and on it goes. Then there are the numerous infomercials, talk shows, and self-help seminars. Where do you turn? Who has the answers? How do you really find balance in life? Is it possible to attain a simpler life?

Yes! It not only is possible but necessary for you to enjoy the things God has to offer you.

VERSES FOR THE DAY

"No one can serve two masters. For you will hate one and love the other; you will be devoted to one and despise the other. You cannot serve both God and money. Matthew 6:24 (NLT)

"Do to others whatever you would like them to do to you. This is the essence of all that is taught in the law and the prophets. Matthew 7:12 (NLT)

Commit your actions to the Lord, and your plans will succeed. Proverbs 16:3 (NLT)

Those who listen to instruction will prosper; those who trust the Lord will be joyful. Proverbs 16:20 (NLT)

Better to be patient than powerful; better to have self-control than to conquer a city. Proverbs 16:32 (NLT)

A prudent person foresees danger and takes precautions. The simpleton goes blindly on and suffers the consequences. Proverbs 27:12 (NLT)

I overheard two older men talking about their health problems at our church. "My new doctor doesn't just treat the symptoms, he treats both the mind and the body."

"Hmmm," the second man grunted, thought for a moment, then asked, "Does he give a discount if the mind is already gone?"
- Clarice Lukenbill, Spencer, IN

It is very unlikely that you will get it right the first, second, or third time that you try to simplify. But just like the tight wire at the circus, there is a safety net under you to catch you when you fall!

Some of you might be thinking that I am like a broken record because I keep using the word priorities throughout these lessons on a simpler life. Well, you are right. I have used this word quite often and do not apologize for it. In order to keep balance in your life, you have to know what is important and make choices based on your priority list.

In the space below, list your priorities in the order of importance in your life.

_____

_____

_____

_____

God should be number one on your priority list. If you keep God first in all that you do, the balancing act will fall into place. He will guide your steps. He will give you wisdom, discernment, and ultimately a balanced life.

So humble yourselves under the mighty power of God, and at the right time he will lift you up in honor. Give all your worries and cares to God, for he cares about you. I Peter 5:6-7 (NLT)

Satan is alive and well and knows your weaknesses.

Stay alert! Watch out for your great enemy, the devil. He prowls around like a roaring lion, looking for someone to devour. Stand firm against him, and be strong in your faith. Remember that your Christian brothers and sisters all over the world are going through the same kind of suffering you are. I Peter 5:8-9 (NLT)

In order to find balance in your life, measure everything against the teachings in the Bible. The Bible is the best resource available to you. Every situation that you come up against will be addressed in God's word. Making time for group Bible studies is also an important step in balancing your life. Spending time with other Christian women will provide true friendships, accountability partners, and Godly counsel.

As you go through this day, ask God to help you look at your situation through His eyes and not your own. Just because we think something should be done a certain way, does not mean it is the only way.

In the space below ask God to help you live this day centered around Him and not centered around you.

_____

_____

_____

Most of the people that you come in contact with today will be looking out for themselves. If you take a different approach and allow God to look out for you, I guarantee that you will have a much better day. When you see others through His eyes and not your own, you remain calm in the midst of your battles and your blood pressure will even remain stable. I am speaking from experience on this issue. When I take God out of the equation, I react in selfish ways. I am easily angered, have no patience for others, and place unreasonable demands on myself and on others.

"God opposes the proud but favors the humble." I Peter 5:5b (NLT)

DAY 3

TWO BASIC PRINCIPLES OF LIFE

VERSES FOR THE DAY

Jesus replied, "'You must love the Lord your God with all your heart, all your soul, and all your mind.' This is the first and greatest commandment. A second is equally important: 'Love your neighbor as yourself.' The entire law and all the demands of the prophets are based on these two commandments." Matthew 22:37-40 (NLT)

No, O people, the Lord has told you what is good, and this is what he requires of you: to do what is right, to love mercy, and to walk humbly with your God. Micah 6:8 (NLT)

"Honor your father and mother. Love your neighbor as yourself." Matthew 19:19 (NLT)

Don't just pretend to love others. Really love them. Hate what is wrong. Hold tightly to what is good. Love each other with genuine affection, and take delight in honoring each other. Never be lazy, but work hard and serve the Lord enthusiastically. Romans 12:9-11 (NLT)

The Bible provides wisdom and understanding for living a simple life. Everything you ever wanted to know about life, but were afraid to ask can be found in the Bible. There are sixty-six books in the Bible. There are thirty-nine books in the Old Testament and twenty-seven books in the New Testament. The Bible that I use as my study Bible consists of one thousand four hundred and six pages. This book has great wisdom and provides comforting passages for anything that you might face in life. It also contains adventure, romance, history, and encouragement.

All Scripture is inspired by God and is useful to teach us what is true and to make us realize what is wrong in our lives. It corrects us when we are wrong and teaches us to do what is right. God uses it to prepare and equip his people to do every good work. 2 Timothy 3:16-17 (NLT)

With all the amazing wisdom and knowledge that God's word possesses, I have discovered that the common thread throughout the Bible is LOVE. The simple truth, the simple life, the simple principles of living are to love God and to love others. If you do this, everything else will fall into place, and you will truly have a simpler life.

When a man and woman fall in love, they try to do everything in a way that pleases the other person. They spend hours getting ready for their dates in order to impress each other. They put up with things that would otherwise irritate them. All for the sake of love.

Love is a powerful thing! Tina Turner had a hit song entitled, "What's Love Got to do With it?" The answer to that question is that love has everything to do with it!!

In the space below, write the words found in I Corinthians 13:13.

_____

_____

_____

THE TWO BASIC PRINCIPLES OF LIFE ARE TO LOVE GOD AND LOVE OTHERS!

1. LOVE GOD!

In order to love God, you need to get to know Him better. The more you know about Him, the more your love will grow. **In the space below, write a prayer asking God to help you find time every day to read His word, pray, and to find ways to grow closer to Him with each passing day.**

_____

_____

_____

Jesus instructs us to love God with all our hearts. What does that mean?

_____

_____

To do something with all your heart, I believe, is to pour your whole being into it the way an athlete pours themselves into training and preparing for an Olympic event. During the training process, which takes years for some, everything that they do revolves around accomplishing the ultimate goal of winning the prize or in this case, the gold medal. Before they eat or drink anything, they must first consider how it will affect their body. They work hard to train every part of their body. In order to achieve such a high goal, they know the training and preparation must consume their daily life. They also realize that every choice that they make will determine the outcome for that day, whether it is good or bad. In other words, " they go at it with their whole heart."

Jesus instructs us to love God with all our souls. What does that mean?

_____

_____

In order to love God with all your soul, there needs to be a deep-rooted desire that comes from within the very depths of your inner being. Instead of just going through the motions and appearing to put Him first in all that you do, this kind of love controls how you feel about life. You look at situations and circumstances the way God teaches in His word and not as the world looks at things. Deep down in the depths of your inner being (soul), you long to please your Creator more than anyone else. You develop a strong desire to know him more and to spend more time in His word and in prayer.

Jesus instructs us to love God with all our minds. What does that mean?

_____

_____

Every action begins as a thought. Every word you say is first formed in your mind. I heard it said that "our minds are like a computer; what goes in is what comes out." There is another quote that says it another way, "garbage in, garbage out." To love God with all your mind is to continuously strive to focus on Him. Take time to recognize the blessings that He has given to you and in turn, be a blessing to others. Actions speak louder than words. There are people that say they love God, but their attitudes and deeds contradict what they are saying. Remember, you have to think it before you can do it. When God is really first in your life, it shows. It shows in your attitude, words, and actions. You begin to take your thoughts captive and control them instead of allowing them to control you. This comes through Bible study and prayer.

Right now, you might be feeling very overwhelmed or inadequate as a Christian because you have not loved God with all your heart, soul, and mind. Don't be so hard on yourself! God loves you unconditionally and understands you better than anyone. He knows your struggles and feels your pain with every passing day. Loving God the way Jesus describes is a work in progress. It does not happen overnight. Just like everything else that we have discussed throughout this study, you need to start with baby steps. One day you will win the prize! The closer you get to this goal, the simpler your life will be.

The key to happiness is obedience, but Satan will do everything he can do to keep you off track. Remember that Satan wants your life to be chaotic. He does not want you to have time for God. It is a constant battle, but the closer you get to God, the easier it is to win the fight!

2. LOVE OTHERS!

The more time you spend with God, the easier it will be to love others the way He instructs in His word.

Imitate God, therefore, in everything you do, because you are his dear children. Live a life filled with love, following the example of Christ. He loved us and offered himself as a sacrifice for us, a pleasing aroma to God.
Ephesians 5:1-2 (NLT)

The keys to loving others are dignity and respect. Learn to treat everyone with dignity and respect. You might not get the same treatment in return, but do it anyway. Remember that God loves you unconditionally, and we are instructed to follow His example in everything that we do.

Recipe for Loving Others
From I Corinthians 13:4-7

Love is patient and kind. Love is not jealous or boastful or proud or rude. It does not demand its own way. It is not irritable, and it keeps no record of being wronged. It does not rejoice about injustice but rejoices whenever the truth wins out. Love never gives up, never loses faith, is always hopeful, and endures through every circumstance.

When we love others the way God wants us to, it removes selfish motives. It also keeps us from thinking of ourselves more highly than we should. It allows us to treat people with the dignity and respect that they deserve. Just because they are not "like us" does not mean they are beneath us or above us. We are equally loved in God's eyes, and we need to see everyone the way He sees them.

LOVING OTHERS GOD'S WAY IS A WORK IN PROGRESS!
In the space below, write a prayer asking God to show you how to love others in a way that will please Him.

_____

_____

I used to spend my summers at Church Camp and one of the highlights each day was "vespers." "Vespers" was the word used for the evening worship service that took place outdoors. We were surrounded by the beauty of God's creation and could sense His presence all around. One of the songs that we sang each night was entitled; "They Will Know We Are Christians By Our Love."

Will "they" know you are a Christian by your love? I have learned some hard lessons in my life. One that I have had to learn over and over again is that if I want a simpler life, the two principles that I need to live by are simply to love God and to love others. I pray that you will learn to live your life this way. It is the only way to experience true joy, peace and contentment!

> *Who in their life hasn't planted a peach pit just hoping that somehow a seedling would grow?*
> *And then they move on to some other adventure, and if it comes up-*
> *Well, they don't even know.*
> *That's one way of picturing your style of living.*
> *You've planted ideas and dreams unaware.*
> *You've noticed somebody whose heart needs attention*
> *And planted a positive feeling in there.*
> *It's part of your nature.*
> *You may not remember the kind and encouraging*
> *Things that you've done...*
> *But everywhere, "peach pits" are growing like crazy,*
> *And people are blooming.*

(A Birthday Card that I received from a friend)

DAY 4
SMOKE AND MIRRORS

I love to host Bible Studies, showers, luncheons, dinners, and dessert nights at my house. I live in a split level home, and I try to make sure that the main floor and the guest bathroom are clean and neat in time for any such events. My husband has been known to rush home from his office in order to dust and vacuum, only to finish just before the doorbell rang and the first guest arrived. If we have had an extremely busy week (Is there any other kind?) and have not de-cluttered the rooms for a while, we sometimes take the piles and put them in a room upstairs and close the door in hopes that no one would open the door and look inside.

A few years ago during the holidays, I hosted a Christmas Tea. I had forty women at this party. I had been so busy getting ready for this special event that I had no time for my regular household routines. My bedroom had become the "catch all" and had many piles placed around the room. In addition to that, the coat closet in the hallway was so full of everything but coats, that when the guests arrived, I had to pile their coats and purses on a bed instead of hanging them in the closet. That's not all...The upstairs portion of my house was so messy that I placed an artificial Christmas tree at the top of the stairs and filled the stairs with stuffed animals so that no one would be able to get up there and see the mess. The main level was decorated beautifully, and everyone had a good time. I'm sure they thought I was just being clever by using my staircase as a unique decoration, but I knew inside that I was really hiding the mess. In reality, it was done in an effort to look like I had everything under control.

VERSES FOR THE DAY

"What sorrow awaits you teachers of religious law and you Pharisees. Hypocrites! For you are so careful to clean the outside of the cup and the dish, but inside you are filthy—full of greed and self-indulgence! You blind Pharisee! First wash the inside of the cup and the dish, and then the outside will become clean, too." Matthew 23:25-26 (NLT)

"What sorrow awaits you teachers of religious law and you Pharisees. Hypocrites! For you are like whitewashed tombs—beautiful on the outside but filled on the inside with dead people's bones and all sorts of impurity. Outwardly you look like righteous people, but inwardly your hearts are filled with hypocrisy and lawlessness. Matthew 23:27-28 (NLT)

But don't just listen to God's word. You must do what it says. Otherwise, you are only fooling yourselves. For if you listen to the word and don't obey, it is like glancing at your face in a mirror. You see yourself, walk away, and forget what you look like. But if you look carefully into the perfect law that sets you free, and if you do what it says and don't forget what you heard, then God will bless you for doing it. James 1:22-25 (NLT)

Just recently, a friend of mine discovered that she had breast cancer and was scheduled for a mastectomy. I invited her over for an evening of girl talk and a banana split (nothing like ice cream to comfort a troubled heart). She reminded me when she arrived that she had never been to my house. I told her that I would give her a tour, but if a door was closed, it meant that room was too messy to show. There were three doors that were closed because of the clutter. When she first walked into my house, it looked as if I had it all together, but then I had to admit that I was hiding my mess behind closed doors.

When you have to shut off rooms because they are so messy, it's time to take a serious look at the situation. If you are like me and tend to hide the mess by putting things in your bedroom, then start by cleaning up and cleaning out in that room before doing anything else. Your bedroom should be a place of serenity, relaxation, and order. However, for most of us, it is just the opposite. I've seen many master bedrooms that look like they are carpeted with clothes and shoes. I have also noticed computers and desks in the master bedroom. It can be very difficult to relax in all the clutter. Especially with a visual reminder that work is not getting done each time you look at the piles of paper on the desk. I would like to suggest that you set aside some time, look at some home décor magazines and make your bedroom a sanctuary.

In the space below, list areas in your house where you are hiding the clutter.

_____

_____

_____

_____

_____

Have you noticed that most people want what they don't have? If a woman has brunette hair, she wants blonde. If a woman has curly hair, she wants straight hair. If she has straight hair, she spends thirty minutes in the mornings curling her hair. If a woman is tall, she wants to be short. If she is short, she wants to appear tall.

Because of the advancements in the fashion world, a woman can actually have whatever look she wants!

I was born a natural redhead with a fair complexion. I am 5'4" in height and have green eyes. Now that I am getting older, my hair color is getting lighter, if you know what I mean. My hairdresser calls those light color strands "non-pigmented". That sounds better than saying that I have gray hairs mixed in with the red! My hair is very course, thick, and straight. When I go to my hairdresser, she blends the different "color tones" in my hair to look more youthful by covering up the non-pigmented hair. Then she uses special scissors that actually thin out the thickness so, as she puts it, I don't look like I am wearing a helmet. Next she layers the hair to give it more movement and bounce. Then she loads me down with products that will enable me to have the same look when I style it at home. I can never make it look like she does, but I am gullible and buy the products every single time. I have been going to the same hairdresser for years, and she says that her job is really like **"smoke and mirrors"**. She gives people the look that they want and makes it appear to be natural when in reality it is very unnatural. She's really good at what she does, and her clients keep coming back for more.

I have the ability to change my complexion by setting up regular visits to a tanning salon. I can make myself appear to be taller by wearing heels. I can even change the color of my eyes by wearing colored contact lens. If I want to take drastic measures, I can set up an appointment with a plastic surgeon and get a new nose, higher cheekbones, larger breasts, a tighter derriere, and the list goes on and on. **It's all smoke and mirrors.**

LOOKING GOOD ON THE OUTSIDE MEANS NOTHING IF YOU LOOK BAD ON THE INSIDE!

How about your heart? Is it right with God? That's the thing that really counts today and everyday! In the space below, write a prayer to God asking Him to show you the areas of your heart that need to be cleaned up and cleaned out.

_____

_____

_____

In today's scripture, Jesus appears to be using some humor as he teaches about this very subject. He calls people that look good on the outside and not on the inside, Hypocrites!

In the space below, write Jesus' words from Matthew 23:25 -26

_____

_____

_____

_____

_____

To simplify means to lighten the load of that which hinders your lifestyle. When you live a double life, one that appears to be one thing when really it is another, do you find yourself hiding things from family and friends? Do you find yourself lying in order to keep up the appearance of good? This can be exhausting and can cause you to have mounted anger, guilt, and bitterness. Just like with the bedroom, we need to start cleaning up and cleaning out today.

In the space below, write the words from James 1:23-24

_____

_____

_____

_____

_____

Look in the mirror and see what things need to be changed. Then ask God to help you make the changes necessary in order to have a simpler life. Don't just look at the outside appearance, but look at the mirror of your soul. Look deep inside, and ask God to reveal your sins to you and to cleanse you of them. Look at James 1:25. We have a promise in God's word that if we do what is right according to God's perfect law, He will bless us.

Be transparent! If you are living life as you should be, then every door of your house can be open, and you will have nothing to hide. If you truly desire to have a simpler life, start cleaning up and cleaning out today. There should be no more need for smoke and mirrors as far as matters of the heart are concerned. I still plan to visit my hairdresser on a regular basis, and that is okay as long as I look good from the inside out and not just on the outside.

Keep putting into practice all you learned and received from me—everything you heard from me and saw me doing. Then the God of peace will be with you.
Philippians 4:9

DAY 5
MAKING IT FUN

VERSES FOR THE DAY

Wherever your treasure is, there the desires of your heart will also be. Matthew 6:21 (NLT)

"Keep on asking, and you will receive what you ask for. Keep on seeking, and you will find. Keep on knocking, and the door will be opened to you. For everyone who asks, receives. Everyone who seeks, finds. And to everyone who knocks, the door will be opened." Matthew 7:7-8 (NLT)

"Anyone who listens to my teaching and follows it is wise, like a person who builds a house on solid rock. Though the rain comes in torrents and the floodwaters rise and the winds beat against that house, it won't collapse because it is built on bedrock. But anyone who hears my teaching and doesn't obey it is foolish, like a person who builds a house on sand. When the rains and floods come and the winds beat against that house, it will collapse with a mighty crash." Matthew 7:24-27 (NLT)

If you need wisdom, ask our generous God, and he will give it to you. He will not rebuke you for asking. But when you ask him, be sure that your faith is in God alone. Do not waver, for a person with divided loyalty is as unsettled as a wave of the sea that is blown and tossed by the wind. Such people should not expect to receive anything from the Lord. Their loyalty is divided between God and the world, and they are unstable in everything they do. James 1:5-8 (NLT)

One of my favorite songs in Children's Church was the song about the wise man and the foolish man. Do you remember that song?

(Form fists with both hands and clap together, one on top of the other.)
> The Wise Man built his house upon the rock,
> The Wise Man built his house upon the rock.
> The Wise Man built his house upon the rock,
> And the rains came tumbling down.

(Move hands and fingers up and down, like rain tumbling down)
> The rains came down and the floods came up.
> The rains came down and the floods came up.
> The rains came down and the floods came up,
> But the house on the rock stood firm!

(Form fists with both hands for building the house and then make the "all gone" motion for sand)
> The Foolish Man built his house upon the sand.
> The Foolish Man built his house upon the sand.
> The Foolish Man built his house upon the sand,
> And the rains came tumbling down.

(Same motions as before)
> The rains came down and the floods came up.
> The rains came down and the floods came up.
> The rains came down and the floods come up,

(Clap hands together when you sing the word "flat")
> And the house on the sand fell flat!

(Same motions as first verse)
> Build your house on the Lord Jesus Christ.
> Build your house on the Lord Jesus Christ.
> Build your house on the Lord Jesus Christ,
> For the house on the Lord stands firm!

I can't remember how old I was when I first learned this song, but it taught me some valuable lessons at a very young age that have gone with me throughout my adult life. It comes from Jesus' teachings in Matthew 7:24–27

The foundation of a simplified life is built on the solid rock of Christ. Placing him at the top of the list each day will allow you to stand firm when the rains and floods of life tumble down.

HUMOR FOR THE DAY
"Knock, knock."
"Who's there?"
"Control freak.
Now you say,
Control freak
who?"

THOUGHT FOR THE DAY
"Spend one hour a day in adoration of the Lord Jesus and you will be all right, you will be content!" - Mother Teresa

**PRAYER FOR
THE DAY**
Dear Heavenly
Father,
Thank you for
this day and for
the blessings of
another day of
life.
Please help me to
simplify my life so
that I may better
serve you.
Help me to
look to you for
guidance in all
that I say and do.
Give me courage
to relinquish
control of my life
and turn it over
to you.
In your son's
name, I pray.
Amen.

When I try to do things my way, my plans often fall apart. When I do things God's way, the plans fall into place and everything runs smoothly.

In the space below, write a prayer to God asking Him to help you let go of the control and give it up to Him.

_____

_____

_____

Look at the list below and place a check by the things you accomplished this week:

___75% of the things on my "to do" list.

___Daily Bible Study

___Daily Prayer

___Laundry (washed, dried, and put away)

___Uninterrupted time with family

___Read a book with a child

___Spent time with a friend

___Eliminated one more unnecessary pile of clutter

___Exercised

___Remembered a friend's birthday

___Arrived on time for more than one appointment

Someone once said that the definition of insanity is doing the same thing over and over again and expecting different results. For many years, I felt like I could have been the poster child for insanity. I kept trying to do things the same way and remained frustrated most of the time because I was constantly running in circles and never really accomplishing anything.

When I began to take a good hard look at the situation, I realized that most of my frustration was coming from a lack of organization in the simplest areas of my life. I was great at organizing big events, and could handle time crunches with ease. My problem was coming from the little things. The phone book was never easy to find when I needed to look up a number. Anytime I needed the church directory or my office directory, it became an all out search that wasted time that could have been spent doing other things. When someone would call and need to leave a message for my husband, I could never find a pen and paper to write the message down. Once I found something to write on and located a pen, I would forget to give the message to my husband and forget where I placed the item (most of the time an old receipt or a napkin) that I wrote it on. These little things had a habit of growing into big things. I knew something had to be done. There was a simple solution to the problem, and I just needed to take time to take care of it.

If you find yourself in a similar situation, there is a simple solution to the problem. Sometimes we just have to get sick and tired of looking for the same thing over and over again before we will do something about it. The solution to my problem was to create a designated place for the phone book, multiple pens, the church directory, the office directory and a phone message book. Using a duplicate phone message book is great because you can write the message on the sheet, tear it off to give to the person needing the message and if it is misplaced, you have it written in the book to refer back to if needed. It's the little things that can make the biggest difference in life!

My designated area is a table with a drawer and a large opening at the bottom where the phone book and yellow pages fit nicely. The directories, phone message book, and pens are located in the drawer. Each time I receive an updated directory or phone book, I remove the old ones so that the area remains uncluttered. No other items are placed on this table, in the drawer or in the large opening. This is the only way to remain organized and efficient in this area. If you do not have a table that you can use, there are other options. Just make sure you have a designated area that remains uncluttered with other things. How many times have you had to tell the person on the other end of the phone to "please hold" while you try and find something to write with and then when you found paper and a pen, the pen was out of ink? This simple solution will solve that problem and help you simplify your life in a big way!

Why not make this a fun project and purchase a used table or one that is unfinished and create a designated message center for your home?

As you come to the close of another unit of study, celebrate!

Plan to spend time with family or friends talking about your newfound freedom. Everyone has worked hard during the week and an evening of fun is well deserved by all! Order pizza, rent a movie, and serve popcorn. Before the pizza arrives, have the children change into their pajamas and bring their pillows and blankets into the family room. Once the pizza arrives, sit at the kitchen table, and have everyone say a prayer of thankfulness to God for the blessings He has given to your family throughout the week. Enjoy the pizza and the funny stories your children will tell about their adventures at school. Take time to tell them about your week and what God has taught you through your Bible Study. Next have the children go into the family room for a family friendly movie and popcorn. If the children are still awake at the end of the movie, serve cookies and milk before sending them to bed. This will be a night to remember for you and your family. If you don't have children at home, borrow some! That's what I do. I love spending time with children, and when I think about celebrating life, I always like to include children because they look at life with innocence and simplicity.

TODAY'S RECIPE

RECIPE FOR A MIDNIGHT SNACK OF COOKIES & MILK

"LEMON COOKIES"
(My son-in-law, Rustin, loves this recipe!)
One box of Lemon Cake Mix
1/3 cup of oil
Two eggs
Combine cake mix, oil, and eggs by hand until fully moistened.
Roll into balls and place on an ungreased cookie sheet.
Slightly flatten balls with bottom of glass (lightly floured).
Bake for 8 minutes at 350 degrees.
Let cool at least one minute before removing from cookie sheet.
Ice with Lemon Frosting

Serve with a cold glass of milk.

GROUP SESSION
WEEK 4

CLEAR THE ROOM – THE REAL ME IS COMING THROUGH!

I. Being _____is an important step toward simplifying your
    _____. Realizing and admitting that _____ that is good
    in your life has come from _____ helps you let go of the
    _____ that belongs to Him.

    Psalm 16:2
    I said to the Lord, "You are my _____! Every _____ thing I
    have comes from _____."

II. God loves you with an _____ love and considers you
    to be the _____ of his eye!

    Psalm 17:8
    Guard me as you would _____ your own _____. Hide me in
    the shadow of your _____.

III. Accepting God's love and loving Him in return will enable you to
     look at things _____. Loving _____
     and loving _____ are the two main principles of a
     _____ life.

     Matthew 22:37-40
     Jesus replied, "'You must _____ the Lord your God with all your
     _____, all your _____, and all your _____.' This is the first
     and greatest commandment. A second is equally _____: 'Love
     your neighbor as _____.' The entire law and all the _____
     of the prophets are based on these two commandments."

WEEK 5

A LIFE ANCHORED IN PURPOSE

When I was eight years old, I remember asking my parents for a blue bicycle. I had seen a blue Schwinn bicycle in a catalog and thought it was the most beautiful bicycle. Christmas was coming soon, and I decided this was the gift I wanted more than anything. I pictured it with a basket on the front and shiny chrome fenders. We lived in a small town in Ohio at the time, and I could ride my bicycle on the sidewalks to visit the elderly women after school. I thought the basket would be great for taking gifts to them. When I told my parents what I wanted, they told me that Santa Claus might not be able to afford it. So I began to pray that Jesus would give Santa Claus the money to buy me the bicycle. My mother overheard my prayers and felt compelled to get the bicycle for me. She didn't tell me that she overheard my prayers until I was an adult. She said they had been teaching me about prayer and also that Jesus was the real reason for the Christmas season - trying not to place too much emphasis on the traditions of Santa Claus. So when she heard me asking Jesus to help Santa, she knew I was beginning to understand. I'm sure the purchase of the bicycle was a huge sacrifice for my parents. I was thrilled with the bicycle and used it as often as possible to visit with the older women in the church. I would always call before visiting them and only stay one hour. I loved my visits and cherish the memories even today. What memories do you cherish from your past?

DAY 1
When Every
Hour is a Rush
Hour

DAY 2
Beside Still
Waters

DAY 3
My Favorite
Things

DAY 4
Sink or Swim

DAY 5
Making it Fun

If we are not careful, life will just zoom right by us, and we won't know what happened. In this fifth unit of study, we will look at ways to slow down, get in tune with God, the Father, and reflect on our favorite things. We will strive to discover our purpose for living as we continue to work towards a simplified life.

In the space below, write a prayer asking God to help you draw closer to him through this week's study.

_____

_____

_____

_____

_____

Anticipate all God wants to teach you this week! Ask Him to show you the things that He wants you to see everyday as you study His word. Be open to a fresh and new approach to life!

DAY 1

WHEN EVERY HOUR IS A RUSH HOUR

Rushing around in order to get things done has caused some funny things to happen. I had a friend tell me about a time when she and her husband, in an effort to save money, were riding to work together. Her husband had to be at work earlier than she did so her morning routine became very rushed. One day she was rushing to feed the dogs, rushing to eat her breakfast, make her lunch, get her daughter ready for school and all of the other things that had to be done before going to work for the day. She took a deep breath, looked around the house one last time and ran to the car. Much to her surprise, she had done quite well except for one important thing...she forgot to put her skirt on. Needless to say, she had to run back into the house and finish getting dressed.

Do you remember when the style was to wear sweaters with shoulder pads? One day a co-worker came rushing into the office wearing her sweater wrong side out. Her shoulder pads were flapping in the wind. She looked like a bird coming in for a landing and didn't even realize what she had done.

Years ago I worked as a Teller at a bank. Fridays were always busy on the Teller Line. One of the tellers rushed to use the restroom in between customers, and when she came out of the restroom, the back of her dress was tucked inside her

VERSES FOR THE DAY

Live wisely among those who are not believers, and make the most of every opportunity. Let your conversation be gracious and attractive so that you will have the right response for everyone.
Colossians 4:5-6 (NLT)

Even while we were with you, we gave you this command: "Those unwilling to work will not get to eat." Yet we hear that some of you are living idle lives, refusing to work and meddling in other people's business. We command such people and urge them in the name of the Lord Jesus Christ to settle down and work to earn their own living. As for the rest of you, dear brothers and sisters, never get tired of doing good.
2 Thessalonians 3:10-13 (NLT)

My child, pay attention to what I say. Listen carefully to my words. Don't lose sight of them. Let them penetrate deep into your heart, for they bring life to those who find them, and healing to their whole body. Guard your heart above all else, for it determines the course of your life.
Proverbs 4:20-23 (NLT)

Look straight ahead, and fix your eyes on what lies before you. Mark out a straight path for your feet; stay on the safe path.
Proverbs 4:25-26 (NLT)

panty hose. The customers at the bank got more than they bargained for that day!

When my daughter was in the first grade her teacher gave all the students an assignment to dress like their favorite character for Storybook Day. She decided to dress like Huckleberry Finn. We got up early that day, painted big freckles on her face, dressed her in overalls, let her go barefooted, put a toy frog in her pocket, gave her a fishing pole to carry, and sent her on her way. She was so cute! Shortly after she arrived at school, I received a phone call from her teacher informing me that Storybook Day was the next week.

Rushing through life can get you into some pretty embarrassing predicaments!

How many hours are you rushing around each day?

___1 hour   ___3 hours   ___5 hours   ___more

What exactly are you rushing to do? _____

_____

When you are rushing to and fro, what frame of mind do you find yourself in?

___impatient   ___angry   ___stressed   ___serious

How can you avoid rushing in the future? _____

_____

The key factor in living a simpler lifestyle is to plan ahead to avoid rushing all the time.

Most women hit the ground rushing from morning to evening. At the end of the day, they couldn't tell you what they had accomplished, if anything. When I find myself doing things at the last minute, I realize later that I didn't even take time to notice the little things that God has placed all around me for my enjoyment. Rushing around causes me to have tunnel vision. I have passed friends on the road and had them tell me later that they saw me and waved, and they could tell that I must have been really busy because I didn't even notice them.

In the space below, write a prayer to God asking him to help you plan ahead.

_____

_____

_____

THOUGHT FOR THE DAY
Said the robin to the sparrow, "Friend, I would really like to know why these anxious human beings rush about and worry so." Said the sparrow to the robin, "Friend, I think that it must be that they have no heavenly father such as cares for you and me."

It is better to over compensate in the area of planning than to under compensate. In order to truly enjoy the blessings received through God, one must choose to live the life out of everyday, NOT zap the life out of everyday!

In the space below write your personal definition of what it means to <u>live the life out of everyday:</u>

_____

_____

_____

For me to live the life out of everyday means to live in a way that pleases God in every way, everyday. I know that in order to do this, I need to plan ahead. I heard it said once that if you fail to plan then you plan to fail. Taking time each day to plan for the next will enable you to rest better at night.

None of us are guaranteed a tomorrow, but if it is God's will for you to live another day, it will be good to have a plan for how you will live the life out of that day.

What sort of things should we plan for? Look at the list below and in the space provided, write the reason that planning for this is an important step toward a simpler life.

Daily Bible Study _____

Daily Prayer Time_____

Set Laundry Days _____

Set Grocery Days_____

Using a Day Planner _____

Balancing the Checkbook _____

Having an Emergency Fund _____

Paying Bills _____

What you will wear the next day _____

I have a very important appointment that I refuse to miss. It is an appointment that is more important than any other. Can you guess what appointment I'm talking about? It is my set appointment with God. I am nothing without Him. When I include Him in my plans, I find ways to live the life out of everyday. I look at every circumstance with a better attitude. I find that I am more disciplined in my actions, my routine, and my overall outlook on life. I don't seem to rush around as much either because I find that spending time with God enables me to find more time in my day to plan ahead. I can't explain it, but I can vouch for it. Try it! Spending time with God has a lifetime guarantee!

I have discovered that you can't out give God. The more time I devote to Him, the more time I seem to have. I know that there are 24 hours in each day. When I spend time with God, I find ways to be more productive and get more out of those 24 hours than I ever did before. I actually find time each day to do something that I enjoy.

If every hour seems like a rush hour then take some time today to evaluate your life. What is controlling you? What changes will you make in order to simplify your life? If you are reacting instead of planning, you will remain in a chaotic state most of the time. In the space below, write a statement about how you plan to start living the life out of everyday, starting today.

_____

_____

_____

_____

DAY 2

BESIDE STILL WATERS

What is it about water that soothes us? Even though the ocean is constantly moving and waves are crashing on the shore, I find it to be calming for my soul. When I walk along a trail that surrounds a lake, I have discovered that my mind drifts and my body begins to relax.

The opposite of rushing is resting. How long has it been since you rested? I'm not talking about a "cat nap" or thirty minutes snoozing on the sofa. I'm talking about the kind of rest mentioned in Psalm 23:1-3. I'm not talking about a vacation that is filled with activities or the occasional Sunday afternoon nap. I'm talking about a day of rest with God. Total solitude.

VERSES FOR THE DAY

The Lord is my shepherd; I have all that I need. He lets me rest in green meadows; he leads me beside peaceful streams. He renews my strength. He guides me along right paths, bringing honor to his name.
Psalm 23:1-3 (NLT)

Because the Lord is my shepherd, I have everything I need! He lets me rest in the meadow grass and leads me beside the quiet streams. He restores my failing health. He helps me do what honors him the most.
Psalm 23: 1-3 (The Living Bible)

The LORD is my shepherd, I lack nothing. He makes me lie down in green pastures, he leads me beside quiet waters, he refreshes my soul. He guides me along the right paths for his name's sake.
Psalm 23:1-3 (NIV)

The Lord is my shepherd; I shall not want. He maketh me to lie down in green pastures; he leadeth me beside the still waters. He restoreth my soul: he leadeth me in the paths of righteousness for his name's sake.
Psalm 23:1-3 (KJV)

**HUMOR FOR
THE DAY**

"Dad, did you go
to Sunday school
when you were
a boy?" "Yes,
my son, I always
went to Sunday
School." "Well, I
think I'm going to
quit; it's not doing
me any good
either."

The Lord is my shepherd, I have everything I need. Psalm 23:1

In the space below, list some of the ways that the Lord provides for your needs.

_____

_____

_____

Larry Burkett, a prominent financial advisor, used to teach people to identify their needs and their wants. He would remind them that God provided everything that was needed.

There are some things that God provides on a daily basis that we take for granted, things such as the air that we breathe, gravity, beauty in nature, and natural resources. He also provides things that we take credit for, such as jobs, houses, health, friends, family, protection, and much more.

To be successful in your efforts to simplify, it is necessary to recognize that God is the provider for you and your family. He provides the means by which you have your needs met. This takes pressure off of you and allows you to enjoy a simpler life.

I have seen firsthand how God provides for those who are faithful to him. My father was diagnosed with terminal cancer at the age of 46. This was very devastating news for our family. On top of dealing with this horrible news, there were economic challenges to face. I prayed everyday, with every ounce of strength I could muster up that God would heal my father. It was not God's will to do so, and my father died at the age of 47. God provided comfort, strength, and healing to my broken heart at a time when I needed it most. He also provided for the financial needs incurred through this ordeal. The surgeon chose to write, "paid in full" on his bill; churches from around the country sent checks to cover other medical expenses as well as funeral expenses. My mother became a house parent at a children's home, which provided her with food, shelter, and a small income. When I read Psalm 23:1, I read it with a thankful heart because I know that it is because of the love my Heavenly Father has for me that I have everything I need!

*He lets me rest in green meadows, he leads me beside peaceful streams.
Psalm 23:2*

Do you like to hike? My husband and I have taken some hiking trips and have grown to love the experience. Fall Creek Falls State Park has some challenging trails that lead to the bottom of a magnificent waterfall. The hike is challenging and tiresome. There are several steep and narrow paths on rocky trails to follow. At the bottom of the trail, it is such a refreshing feeling to sit and enjoy the beauty all around and to experience rest beside the stream. The only problem with this adventure is that you have to hike back up the steep hills and back over the rocky trails in order to get back to the car. There is only one way in and one way out.

I think this verse of scripture is like the hiking trail at Fall Creek Falls State Park and very much like life itself. The experiences that we face in life are sometimes challenging and tiresome. There are times when we are struggling to fight an uphill battle and other times when we are experiencing rocky relationships. In the midst of our hectic lifestyles, God offers us times to rest and places to experience peace. Most of us don't take time to pay attention to the rest and relaxation that God has to offer.

In the space below, write a prayer to God asking him to help you recognize the times that you need to rest.

_____

_____

_____

He renews my strength. He guides me along right paths, bringing honor to his name. Psalm 23:3

I long for my alone times with God. It is in time spent with him that I find my strength for the things that I am facing in my everyday life. Spending time alone in his word with no interruptions, allows me to focus on his purpose for my life.

If there is anyway that you can find time to be alone with God for a whole day, I promise it will change your life! I know this seems like a weird concept and might seem awkward at first, but after a few minutes, you will sense his presence with you and feel comfort and peace surrounding you.

I like to find a place of solitude that allows me to pray out loud or to sing praises to God. I will usually have a journal with me in case I decide to write prayers, poetry, experiences, or goals for future reference.

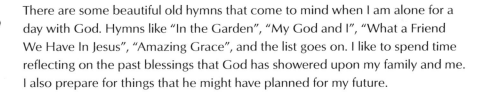

There are some beautiful old hymns that come to mind when I am alone for a day with God. Hymns like "In the Garden", "My God and I", "What a Friend We Have In Jesus", "Amazing Grace", and the list goes on. I like to spend time reflecting on the past blessings that God has showered upon my family and me. I also prepare for things that he might have planned for my future.

Spending a day alone with God allows you to formulate a plan that will enable you to continue to set goals that are in line with his plan and help you simplify your life. In doing this, he will show you the things that should matter most to you and help you prioritize your life.

It's true that you can lead a horse to water, but you can't make him drink. In the same way, God leads us to still and peaceful waters, but it is up to us to accept his offer to rest.

When was the last time you spent more than an hour with God?

_____

When I have an important decision to make, I always make it a point to spend a day alone with God before making the decision. I find a place where I can reflect on the beauty of his creation. I read the Bible, journal, pray, and meditate as I seek his guidance. Just as Psalm 23:3 says, He really does guide me along the right paths when I take the time to seek his plan for my life.

It is my prayer that you will take time out of your hectic schedule and make an appointment with your Heavenly Father. It will be a life changing experience. One that is difficult to explain, but well worth the time and effort it takes to plan it.

The secret to a simpler life is found in time spent alone with God.

DAY 3
MY FAVORITE THINGS

One of my favorite movies of all time is *The Sound of Music*. In this movie, Maria is working as a nanny to seven children. One day the children are feeling very down and she tries to cheer them up by getting them to think about their favorite things. Some of their favorite things were raindrops on roses and whiskers on kittens, brown paper packages tied up with strings, snowflakes that fell on their nose and eyelashes, silver white winters that melt into spring. As the song goes, these were a few of their favorite things.

VERSES FOR THE DAY

And now, dear brothers and sisters, one final thing. Fix your thoughts on what is true, and honorable, and right, and pure, and lovely, and admirable. Think about things that are excellent and worthy of praise. Keep putting into practice all you learned and received from me—everything you heard from me and saw me doing. Then the God of peace will be with you.
Philippians 4:8-9 (NLT)

How precious are your thoughts about me, O God. They cannot be numbered! I can't even count them; they outnumber the grains of sand! And when I wake up, you are still with me!
Psalm 139:17-18 (NLT)

Joyful is the person who finds wisdom, the one who gains understanding. For wisdom is more profitable than silver, and her wages are better than gold.
Proverbs 3:13-14 (NLT)

HUMOR FOR THE DAY
From the book, Kids Talk About God:
In the Garden of Eden, why did the devil tempt Eve instead of Adam?

Rachel, 9: "Because Satan is a boy and boys don't like girls."

Katie, 11: "Eve hadn't lived there as long as Adam."

Victoria, 8: "Eve was just walking around, and I think Adam was busy."

In the space below, list some of your favorite things:

_____

_____

As you work on ways to simplify your life, take time to focus on your favorite things.

Whatever is good and perfect comes down to us from God our Father, who created all the lights in the heavens. He never changes or casts a shifting shadow. He chose to give birth to us by giving us his true word. And we, out of all creation, became his prized possession. James 1:17–18 (NLT)

Wow, did you catch that? Out of all creation, we are his choice possession! When God thinks of his favorite things, he thinks about you and me!

In the song, "My Favorite Things", there is a line that goes like this: "When the dog bites, when the bee stings, when I'm feeling sad, I simply remember my favorite things, and then I don't feel so bad." This is a great prescription for the blues. When you feel down about something, offset it with something positive. Instead of focusing on the bad in someone or something, make every effort to find something good in them. Instead of dwelling on the bad news around you, think of reasons to be joyful. I've heard it said that if Momma ain't happy, ain't nobody happy. To make life simpler for all those around you, choose to be happy.

Happiness is a choice. You can't always change the circumstances, but you can determine how you will react to the situation. Just like in the song, when the dog bites or when the bee stings you need to think on your favorite things, and then you won't feel so bad!

One of my favorite things is to know the Savior. It is important to know him personally and intimately. Knowing that I am one of his choice possessions is such an encouragement to me. I hope you will feel the same way too!

He loves us so much that he is delaying his return so that as many as will accept him will have a chance before it is too late.

In the space below, write the words found in 2 Peter 3:8-9.

_____

_____

When I think of my favorite things, I am reminded that God owns everything in Heaven and on earth. He has placed all things here for us to enjoy. That's how much He loves you and that's how much He loves me.

If you are struggling to simplify your life, just look around at all the numerous things God has given to you. Take time to enjoy some of your favorite things. In the space below, write a prayer to God thanking Him for every good and perfect gift that He has given to you.

_____

_____

Take time each day to enjoy your favorite things. As my father used say, "You only live once, don't be miserable while you are here. Live everyday as if it might be your last day on this earth because it just might be." What wonderful words of wisdom! I try and live my life like this each and every day. Find reasons to be happy even on the worst of days. I have so many favorite things; so I should have at least another 100 years to live the life out of everyday! How about you?"

In the space below, write down three areas where you could use an attitude adjustment:

_____

_____

_____

Now go out there today and live the life out of this day! Life is too short to make it so complicated. Live a simpler life, and enjoy some of your favorite things!

PRAYER FOR THE DAY
Dear Heavenly Father,
Thank you for giving me so many wonderful things to enjoy. Thank you for making me your choice possession. Give me guidance as I strive to simplify my life so that I may better serve you.
In your son's name, I pray.
Amen.

DAY 4
SINK OR SWIM

VERSES FOR THE DAY

As the Scriptures say, "People are like grass; their beauty is like a flower in the field. The grass withers and the flower fades. But the word of the Lord remains forever." And that word is the Good News that was preached to you.
I Peter 1:24-25 (NLT)

Devote yourselves to prayer with an alert mind and a thankful heart.
Colossians 4:2 (NLT)

A final word: Be strong in the Lord and in his mighty power. Put on all of God's armor so that you will be able to stand firm against all strategies of the devil. For we are not fighting against flesh-and-blood enemies, but against evil rulers and authorities of the unseen world, against mighty powers in this dark world, and against evil spirits in the heavenly places. Therefore, put on every piece of God's armor so you will be able to resist the enemy in the time of evil. Then after the battle you will still be standing firm.
Ephesians 6:10-13 (NLT)

In Atlanta, Georgia, there is a water park called, Whitewater. At this park there are water slides for the fearless at heart, inner tube rides on rough waters and calm waters. I love to go to Whitewater because there is something for everyone to enjoy. The most popular attraction is the Wave Pool. At times it looks like an average pool of water that is five feet deep. It is not unusual to see people relaxing on inner tubes throughout the day. In a matter of seconds, the calm waters change to a pool of high waves that move across the water continuously for fifteen minutes at a time. When the waves start, people swarm to the pool for the thrill of the inner tube ride. Being the cheapskate that I am, I decided not to rent an inner tube and just ride the waves like I do in the ocean. The difference however, is that these waves are continuous, and at the beach, they come in cycles. As the waves came, the currents began to pull me deeper and deeper into the center of the pool, and I found myself being pushed under the water and covered by a multitude of people on inner tubes. Each time I would try and come to the top, another wave of water, and inner tubes would push me back under. I was convinced that I was going to drown. I was able to work my way over to the side of the pool as I continued gasping for air just before going under again. Finally, a Life Guard saw me and came to my rescue. Just seconds after I was pulled out of the water, the waves were turned off, and the waters were calm once again. This experience was very scary for me. I was fighting for my life while everyone around me was having the time of their lives, and for what seemed to be a very long time, no one even noticed.

Do you feel like you are drowning? When you look at your "to do" list, do you feel overwhelmed? Do you hear yourself taking big sighs throughout the day as you come up for air? If so, it's time to get serious about ways to cut back. I would like to offer you a life preserver, an instrument that will enable you to stay above water.

Do you remember an old television show called *Gilligan's Island*? In one of the episodes, Gilligan is out exploring on the island and steps into some quick sand. He immediately starts to sink. The Skipper is looking for Gilligan and ends up in the same quick sand. They try to get out, but they keep sinking deeper. The Professor finally comes along and figures out a scientific solution to the problem and gets them out of the sand before they go completely under.

Do you feel like you are sinking? Are you in debt over your head? Are you looking at your situation and thinking the only way out is to declare bankruptcy? Don't do it! There is a better way. I would like to offer you a life preserver, an instrument that will enable you to be pulled out of the sinking sand.

In the space below, list the things that cause you to have a drowning or sinking feeling.

_____

_____

_____

How did you get into the shape you are in right now?

_____

_____

_____

Sometimes it is because of circumstances beyond our control that we end up experiencing these times of trouble. The company that you work for decides to "down size" and you don't make the cut. Illness comes into the family and all of your time and energy is devoted to caring for them. You have an accident and are not able to work for an extended period of time. Your children are involved in so many activities that there is no time for housework. There are so many things that can come into our lives unexpectedly that can overtake us if we allow them to do so.

HUMOR FOR THE DAY
Bumper Sticker: SO MUCH WORK...So few women to do it.

THOUGHT FOR THE DAY
You grow up on the day you have your first real laugh at yourself.
– Ethel Barrymore

In most circumstances, if you have a budget in place, you will be able to stay afloat and not have to feel as if you are drowning. I know for some people, the word budget makes them cringe, but it can allow you to have restful nights in the midst of a storm.

To budget simply means to plan ahead.

1. Budget your finances. As Dave Ramsey says, "Live on less than you make." Find ways to build an emergency fund that will keep you afloat if you lose your job or have to be out of work for an extended period of time. Most people seem to be living from paycheck to paycheck, and when something unexpected happens, they are sunk due to poor planning. Dave Ramsey, of Financial Peace University, teaches people to have a minimum of three months expenses set aside in an emergency fund.

If you have debt, then the next important step is to map out a plan to reduce your debt and to ultimately be debt free. *Just as the rich rule the poor, so the borrower is servant to the lender. Proverbs 22:7 (NLT)* When you owe a debt of any kind, the lending institution controls how you use your money. The sooner you can get out of debt, the better off you will be. Filing bankruptcy is not the answer. You agreed in good faith to repay the debt, and filing bankruptcy is going back on your word, and in reality you are stealing. There are other options, and lenders will work with you. I have found that most of the time when a person files for bankruptcy or borrows against their home, they experience a brief period of relief and then get right back in the same shape. The action taken served as a band-aid, but did not fix the problem. God's way is much better. Just like with everything else in life, when we try and do it our way, our lives will remain out of control. His way is always better.

If you are struggling in the area of finances, I recommend that you contact a Christian Financial Counselor. For more information on this, check with your local church, Christian Radio Station, or Christian Bookstore. There are numerous resources available to you.

2. Budget your time. Instead of reacting all day long, have a plan. When you have a plan in place, even the unexpected events that occur will not shake you. You can simply look at your schedule for the day and decide what can be rearranged or postponed. A Day Planner is one of the best tools you can have when budgeting your time. I use a pencil when filling in my daily calendar. I have learned that nothing is ever set in stone. Unexpected things occur most everyday. I have a set appointment with God every day, and the only reason that I would ever change it would be for a dire emergency. Spending an hour with God each day gives me an inner peace that keeps me sane throughout the day.

Budgeting your time will also allow you to discover ways to be more efficient in your daily household chores. When you write down the things that you do on a regular basis, you will begin to see areas that could be considered "time wasters". Multi-tasking is what women do best, but there is always room for improvement. Did you know that when you brush your teeth, you can also be cleaning off the counter, putting away clothes, or making up your bed? I realized several years ago that it takes me three minutes to brush my teeth, but I am only using one hand. This means that my other hand is free to do other things during that time. I have cut my morning routine down by three minutes by multi-tasking while brushing my teeth. Now I realize that for some of you that may seem to be going a little overboard, but for me, it works! When you know ahead of time all the things that you need to do in a day, it allows you to plan ahead, get things done and have time for the things that you enjoy most.

A budget is like an inner tube–it keeps you from sinking!

After having such a scary adventure at Whitewater in Atlanta, you would think I would have learned my lesson. However, the very next time that we decided to go to the water park, I ended up doing the same thing again. I know what you are thinking, and I agree, "That was pretty dumb!" But how many times do we do the same things over and over and find ourselves gasping for air or sinking again? The good news is that God allows us to have a fresh new start anytime we want one and continues to guide us along the way. We simply have to ask. Life will be so much simpler when we finally realize this and do things His way! Will we ever get it? With God's help, the answer is, YES!

In the space below, write a prayer to God asking him to guide your steps along the way as you strive for a simpler life.

_____

_____

_____

The Lord is my strength and shield.
I trust him with all my heart.
He helps me, and my heart is filled with joy.
I burst out in songs of thanksgiving.
Psalm 28:7 (NLT)

DAY 5
MAKING IT FUN

VERSES FOR THE DAY

Always be joyful. Never stop praying. Be thankful in all circumstances, for this is God's will for you who belong to Christ Jesus.
I Thessalonians 5:16-18 (NLT)

Don't be concerned about the outward beauty of fancy hairstyles, expensive jewelry, or beautiful clothes. You should clothe yourselves instead with the beauty that comes from within, the unfading beauty of a gentle and quiet spirit, which is so precious to God.
I Peter 3:3-4 (NLT)

A little extra sleep, a little more slumber, a little folding of the hands to rest—then poverty will pounce on you like a bandit; scarcity will attack you like an armed robber.
Proverbs 6:10-11 (NLT)

First impressions are lasting impressions. What kind of impression do you make when someone comes into your home for the first time? Do they feel that they are welcome or an interruption? Take a look around your home today, and try to imagine what others may feel when they come into your home. Then decide what changes you might need to make in an effort to give your home more warmth and, you guessed it, fun.

Your home should reflect your interests and personality. If you are a creative person, then don't be afraid to express your creativity in your décor. Be bold and brighten up a room with a fresh coat of paint. If you prefer to decorate with more traditional whites and tans, then add a pillow or picture with colors that brighten up a room. I get most of my decorating ideas from magazines. I thumb through the pages until I find something that catches my eye. It's a great way to find ways to update your home without hiring a designer and depleting the bank account.

My husband and I decided to update our décor and found some color schemes that were bold but beautiful. Before the color change we had a brown paneled den, a white kitchen, an off-white dining room and living room, and outdated wallpaper in our foyer. We both have outgoing personalities and decided to reflect that in our new colors. We now have a yellow den and kitchen, a red dining room, a brown living room, and a beautiful brown textured foyer. Just adding the new colors to the walls, changed the looks of our home completely. After finishing the project, I had a "Girlfriend Gathering" at my house on a Saturday morning. One of my girlfriends walked in and said, "Wow, I feel like I just walked into a showroom!"

Once you have de-cluttered a room, try updating it with something new. It doesn't have to be as drastic as a new coat of paint. It can be a new cluster of pictures or a mirror. Do something that says, "welcome" in every room of your house.

In the space below, list some areas of your home that could use a face lift.

_____

_____

_____

As you simplify your schedule, find ways to incorporate some time for fun decorating projects. Just like everything that we have discussed in the past few weeks, it is best to do this one room at a time and as you have the money to pay for it.

"Girlfriend Gatherings" can be fun. In celebration of completing another week of study, why not invite some friends over for coffee, cake, and girl talk? Tell them about your efforts to simplify, and ask them for decorating ideas. Better yet, let them help you clean out a closet. They won't be attached to the "stuff" like you are and will have no problem helping you get rid of things. It might even inspire them to go home and start doing the same thing at their house.

If you are a pack rat, ask yourself "why?" Do you ever think you will have use for the things you are holding on to? Right now the styles in fashion are much like the styles of past decades. I hear women say that they wish they had saved all of their clothes from the past, since styles seem to always come back around. I really don't want to burst your bubble, but do you really need to be wearing those same styles again? If you are holding on to outdated clothes in hopes that you can wear them again, I suggest that you get rid of them, and make room for new things. Let go! It will be okay. Don't let go of everything at once. Take it one step at a time.

It can be so refreshing to step back from chaos and realize there is light at the end of the tunnel for all to enjoy!

HUMOR FOR THE DAY
Courtroom lawyer, questioning a potential juror:
Q: Have you lived in this town all your life?
A: Not yet!

THOUGHT FOR THE DAY
Create a focal point for any room, and give it visual appeal.

In the space below write down accomplishments you have made toward reaching your goal to simplify.

_____

_____

_____

As you celebrate life, do something for someone else today. I have found that when I do something good for someone else, I feel better about myself. Call a friend that is going through a rough time; send an encouraging card to a friend that just lost a job; raise money for a worthy cause, or offer a helping hand at church for an hour.

In the space below, write a prayer to God asking him to show you ways to encourage others today.

_____

_____

_____

Celebrate life by living a God-centered life and not a self-centered life!

Take some time to relax, and reflect on what God is showing you through this SIMPLIFY Bible Study. Several years ago I attended a teacher's conference in Georgia. The conference was held two days before Thanksgiving, and the main topic of conversation for most was their plans for the holiday. It was my year to host the Family Thanksgiving Dinner, and I needed some ideas for desserts. One of the women at the table told me about a cake recipe that had become a part of their holiday tradition. She had used this recipe for so many years that she didn't even have to refer to a recipe card to tell me how to prepare it. So I wrote the recipe on a napkin and tried it out on my family that year. It has now become one of my family's favorites and a holiday tradition for us too. Thanks to Mae Brown of Elberton, Georgia, I present you with the recipe for SPOON COCONUT CAKE:

TODAY'S RECIPE

SPOON COCONUT CAKE
(Use a 9x13 glass dish)

One box of Deluxe Yellow Cake Mix (Duncan Hines)
Bake according to directions on the box.
Let cake cool.

In a sauce pan place the following:
2 cups of milk
1 cup of sugar
1 cup of coconut
Bring to a boil.
Let cool.
Spoon mixture over cake.

Icing: Spread cool whip on top of cake then cover with coconut.

This dessert is delicious served with coffee or hot tea!

GROUP SESSION
WEEK 5

SHHH – I'M TRYING TO REST!

I.   There is no need to _____. God is in _____.
     He provides _____ for the _____ and _____ for his people.

     Psalm 29:10 -11
     The Lord _____ over the floodwaters.
     The _____ reigns as king _____. The Lord gives his _____
     strength. The Lord _____ them with peace.

II. Without _____ we will become ineffective in our _____. If _____ ain't
     happy, ain't _____ happy! Sometimes the best thing for us is a _____.!

     Isaiah 40:30
     Even youths will become _____ and _____, and young men
     will fall in exhaustion.

III. Psalm 23:2-3
     He lets me _____ in green meadows; he leads me beside _____
     streams He _____ my _____. He guides me along right
     paths, bringing _____ to his name.

     Spending quiet time with God is an important step in simplifying your life.
     He provides rest for the weary, strength for each day, and a peace that
     surpasses our understanding.

WEEK 6

A LIFE ANCHORED IN TRUTH

When I am riding in the car, I love to listen to the radio. Music is a gift from God for all to enjoy. I have pulled up behind people and noticed that they too were enjoying some music on the radio. They are dancing and singing and clapping their hands and simply enjoying life. They don't seem to care that others are watching. I often wonder if they even realize that they can be seen. Others enjoy their music by thumping the bass so loudly that it literally shakes the cars around them. I try to remain civil when listening to the radio, but I do love to sing along. Every once in a while in the middle of one of my favorite songs an interruption will occur. A long high-pitched sound will be the only thing playing on the radio. After 30-60 seconds of this ear piercing sound, an announcer will say, "This was a test of the Emergency Broadcast System. This was only a test. Should an emergency occur, you would be instructed at that time as to what to do in the event of a real emergency. Again, this was only a test. We now return you to your regularly scheduled radio program." For you and for me, there will be days when it is just a test and other days when a real emergency will occur. It is much easier to face those emergency situations if you have learned to simplify.

In this sixth unit of study, we will look at ways to simplify and prepare for the interruptions that come along with everyday life. We will also discuss ways to accept and react to those unexpected circumstances that are beyond our control.

Anticipate all God wants to teach you this week! Ask Him to show you the things He wants you to see everyday as you study His word. Be open to a fresh new approach to life!

DAY 1
Enough is
Enough

DAY 2
The Main
Thing

DAY 3
Feeling Good

DAY 4
Sweet Dreams

DAY 5
Making it Fun

DAY 1
ENOUGH IS ENOUGH

What do people really get for all their hard work? I have seen the burden God has placed on us all. Yet God has made everything beautiful for its own time. He has planted eternity in the human heart, but even so, people cannot see the whole scope of God's work from beginning to end. So I concluded there is nothing better than to be happy and enjoy ourselves as long as we can. And people should eat and drink and enjoy the fruits of their labor, for these are gifts from God. Ecclesiastes 3:9-13 (NLT)

God blesses you who are hungry now, for you will be satisfied. God blesses you who weep now, for in due time you will laugh. Luke 6:21 (NLT)

Not that I was ever in need, for I have learned how to be content with whatever I have. I know how to live on almost nothing or with everything. I have learned the secret of living in every situation, whether it is with a full stomach or empty, with plenty or little. Philippians 4:11-12 (NLT)

Don't love money; be satisfied with what you have. For God has said, "I will never fail you. I will never abandon you." So we can say with confidence, "The Lord is my helper, so I will have no fear. What can mere people do to me?" Hebrews 13:5-6 (NLT)

I attended a conference in Tampa, Florida, and one evening I had dinner with a professional organizer. One of her specialties is closet design. We had a very interesting conversation. In talking with her that night, I learned that the average woman owns ninety pairs of shoes. Ninety pairs of shoes! Another woman at the table overheard the conversation and leaned over to me and whispered, "I have one hundred and twenty pairs. I counted them just before I left to come to the conference." Well, when I returned home, I informed my husband that I was a "below average woman" because I didn't have nearly enough shoes in my closet! Ninety pairs of shoes? Why?

I love purses. When I go shopping, I tend to gravitate toward the handbag section. Recently I had to purchase some panty hose, and the only cashier available was in the handbag section of the store. It took every ounce of willpower that I could muster up just to look and not buy another handbag. There are so many new colors, shapes and sizes! I have a nice variety of purses now, so I have to ask myself, "How many purses does one really need?"

Collecting teacups and saucers has been a hobby of mine for years. I enjoy going to antique shops and finding unique teacups and saucers. My cabinets are overrun with a vast assortment of antique and unique cups and saucers. Last year, I actually gave some away so that I could buy more. Why?

I know a man that collects Fossil watches. He has drawers full of these watches and doesn't even wear a watch. I asked him about it one day, and he told me that watches irritate his wrist so he doesn't like to where them. Why does he need drawers full of watches?

There are women that subscribe to four or more magazines a month. They don't really have time to read that many magazines so they put them in a stack with the intentions of reading them later. Before they get around to reading them, the next month's issue is in the mailbox. Yet it seems that every time the subscriptions come up for renewal, they order them once again. Why?

In the space below, write down the items that you stockpile.

_____

_____

_____

In the space below answer this question: Why do you have so many?

_____

_____

When is enough, enough?

There is nothing wrong with having nice things and collecting items that interest you. It becomes a problem when it interferes with your life and begins to complicate it. In looking at ways to simplify life, a good place to start is by assessing your situation and deciding where you might need to cut back on your purchases. When you are buying things that you don't need you, are spending money that could be put to better use. You are also taking up space that could be used for other things. If your collectibles are overtaking your household it's time to cut back.

THOUGHT
FOR THE DAY
A friend is always
loyal, and a
brother is born
to help in time of
need.
Proverbs 17:17
(NIV)

Be loving even
at times when
you're correcting
a child or
complaining to a
store clerk.

In the space below, write a prayer to God asking him to help you keep your possessions in check.

_____

_____

_____

I have discovered a different way of enjoying my collectibles. In order to make room for another, I share with other people. Last year I went through my cabinet and found teacups that reminded me of different people and gave them to my friends as gifts. Because they know how much I enjoy tea and tea parties, these gifts hold sentimental value to them. I have received emails and phone calls from several of my girlfriends telling me that they were enjoying a delicious cup of hot tea and thinking of me.

If I can't justify buying another purse for myself, I think of someone else that might like to have a new funky purse or a classy sleek one. Then I make the purchase to be used for a Christmas or birthday gift.

When I buy a gift for someone, I like to buy things that I would like to have for myself. It makes shopping more fun, and if they know me, they know they are getting something that will remind them of our friendship each time they use it.

At Christmas time, I hear the word "re-gift" quite often. It's not a bad idea to re-gift if the item is in good shape or of sentimental value. For most people, it will mean more to them if they receive something from you that has special meaning and value than if you spend money that you don't really need to spend.

As you look around your house today, think of ways to de-clutter, and in the space below try and answer today's question: When is enough enough?

_____

_____

_____

What about the people that seem to always want a newer and better car or a bigger house? I understand that there comes a time when the one bedroom apartment just won't do anymore, but how many people really need to live in houses with 10,000 square feet? I enjoy touring new homes for decorating ideas, and recently I toured six homes that were on display in Nashville. The smallest home was 7,800 square feet and the largest was over 10,000 square feet. The homes were magnificent! I find it hard to imagine that anyone would really need that much room. In some of the homes, I felt like I was at a hotel. There is nothing wrong with having a house like that, but I would find it hard to justify a reason to do so. I wonder how many people would become dissatisfied with this too and want an even bigger house?

In the space below, write the words from I Timothy 6:7-10

_____

_____

_____

_____

_____

_____

_____

If accumulating stuff is the driving force of your life, you will never be satisfied.

In order to simplify, you must learn to be satisfied!

PRAYER FOR THE DAY
Dear Heavenly Father,
Thank you for all of my blessings. Help me to be satisfied, and show me ways to simplify my life. Help me to have a generous heart and to be mindful of others. In your son's name, I pray. Amen.

DAY 2
THE MAIN THING

VERSES FOR THE DAY

So humble yourselves before God. Resist the devil, and he will flee from you. Come close to God, and God will come close to you. Wash your hands, you sinners; purify your hearts, for your loyalty is divided between God and the world. Let there be tears for what you have done. Let there be sorrow and deep grief. Let there be sadness instead of laughter, and gloom instead of joy. Humble yourselves before the Lord, and he will lift you up in honor.
James 4:7-10 (NLT)

Let us hold tightly without wavering to the hope we affirm, for God can be trusted to keep his promise. Let us think of ways to motivate one another to acts of love and good works. And let us not neglect our meeting together, as some people do, but encourage one another, especially now that the day of his return is drawing near.
Hebrews 10:23-25 (NLT)

"For God loved the world so much that he gave his one and only Son, so that everyone who believes in him will not perish but have eternal life. God sent his Son into the world not to judge the world, but to save the world through him.
John 3:16-17 (NLT)

How many times have you run into the grocery store to buy a gallon of milk and come out of the store with no less than three sacks of groceries? When that happens, I hear myself saying, "The main thing that I needed was milk, but I ended up spending $50.00!"

When I am at a gathering of women and see a girlfriend on the other side of the room, I will think of something that I need to tell her and rush over to talk to her. Just as most women will do, we begin talking and later on in the evening, I realize that I forgot to tell her the main thing that I went over to tell her.

Do you see how easily distracted we become? It can happen so quickly. The main thing for us to do each day is to love God above everything else and to keep him first in all that we do. Even in striving to do this, we get distracted.

Making time for God each day is the key element for a simpler life!

As you make your "to do" list for each day, make sure that you include time alone with God on the list. I have found that if I am not careful, even my time alone with God gets filled with distractions. So the first thing I do is say a prayer asking God to help me block out everything around me and focus on the things He wants to show me through His word and through prayer. I love to write and journaling is one of the ways that I block out distractions around me. I write scriptures down in my journal, and then beneath the scripture verse, I write a prayer about that verse. This also allows me to go back later and see how God blessed me and carried me through the day. I have journals dating back to 1994, neatly tucked away of course, and I refer back to them from time to time as a source of encouragement.

What about church services on Sunday mornings? Do you have a hard time getting everyone ready to go? What is your attitude like before you get there? I venture to say that a high percentage of families have argued about something before pulling into the parking lot of the church building. They have forgotten that the main thing they are going to do is show honor to God and commune with fellow Christians around the table that was prepared in remembrance of our Savior, Jesus Christ.

Bob Russell of Southeast Christian Church in Louisville, Kentucky, spoke at a leadership conference that I attended years ago, and he emphasized throughout his message that in order to succeed as a leader for Christ, we must make the main thing - the main thing in everything that we say and do. You might have to read that statement again for it to make sense, but it is simply put. It's another way of saying, "stay focused."

In the space below, write a prayer to God asking him to help you to stay focused today on the main thing.

_____

_____

_____

Remember that Satan specializes in ways to bring you down. If you keep God first in your life, there is no room for Satan. The Bible teaches us that if we resist Satan, he will flee from us. It is much easier to resist the temptations that he throws at us when we are holding hands with our Heavenly Father. Even though I am getting older by the day, I still like to picture myself as one of God's little girls. When I am scared, discouraged, sad, or confused, I close my eyes and picture him scooping me up and placing me on his lap. I like to think he is rocking me back and forth. He whispers in my ear that he loves me and

HUMOR FOR THE DAY
There are three ways to get something done:
1. Do it yourself.
2. Hire someone to do it.
3. Forbid your kids to do it.

that everything will be okay. We are told in scripture that God loves us so much that He sent his only son to die on a cross for our sins. He offers comfort and peace when we need it most. We simply need to stay connected through daily Bible Study and prayer.

God is my father, and I am his child. I guess that makes me a Daddy's Girl!

Attending church services on Sundays should be the highlight of your week. It is a time to see friends in Christ, a place of encouragement and re-commitment and a glimpse of what Heaven will be like. Hopefully you will hear laughter and feel genuine concern for others all around you. The seats are filled with imperfect people, just like you, that are striving to have a closer walk with God. If attending church services has become more of an obligation than a joy, pray that God will help you change your attitude. Instead of feeling like an obligation, it should feel like an honor. When this mind shift occurs, you will look forward to attending, and it will become a top priority for you.

Have you heard the old saying, "If Momma ain't happy, ain't nobody happy?" Women set the tone for most everything around them. If you look forward to Sunday services, then your family will too. If you have been in a habit of making this event a chore for the entire family, it will take a while for them to change their way of thinking....try it!

In the space below write down five things that you can do ahead of time to be better prepared for Sunday services.

PRAYER FOR THE DAY
Dear Heavenly Father,
Thank you for reminding me that I am your child.
Help me to keep you first in all that I say and do.
Help me to simplify my life so that I may better serve you.
In your son's name, I pray.
Amen.

_____

_____

_____

_____

DAY 3
FEELING GOOD

How do you feel today? Do you feel that you are learning to simplify? Do you feel like you are making progress in de-cluttering your home, your heart, and your mind? If you feel good about the changes you have made and the strides that you have reached toward your goals, then remember it is through Bible study and prayer that you have found this refreshing approach to life.

One of the pitfalls that people fall into when they start feeling good about their accomplishments is that they forget who brought them to this point and start depending on their own strength once again. Before you know it, they are right back where they started.

I see this in areas of finance, weight, organization, and addictions. When this happens, we end up starting the cycle all over again. I want to caution you not to get so puffed up about your progress that you feel you don't need God's help anymore. It's great to feel good and to want to improve, but make sure that you give credit where credit is due. It is through Him that you are discovering this newfound freedom.

God cares about everything in your life. You can feel good about the fact that he will be there to catch you anytime you fall.

VERSES FOR THE DAY

Trust in the Lord with all your heart; do not depend on your own understanding. Proverbs 3:5 (NLT)

For I was hungry, and you fed me. I was thirsty, and you gave me a drink. I was a stranger, and you invited me into your home. I was naked, and you gave me clothing. I was sick, and you cared for me. I was in prison, and you visited me.' "Then these righteous ones will reply, 'Lord, when did we ever see you hungry and feed you? Or thirsty and give you something to drink? Or a stranger and show you hospitality? Or naked and give you clothing? When did we ever see you sick or in prison and visit you?'

"And the King will say, 'I tell you the truth, when you did it to one of the least of these my brothers and sisters, you were doing it to me!' Matthew 25:35-40 (NLT)

Pride goes before destruction, and haughtiness before a fall. Proverbs 16:18 (NLT)

It can be difficult to stay on task everyday. Have you noticed how quickly an organized drawer can become unorganized again? You may spend an entire day cleaning out a closet and in a matter of days, find it messy again. Our lives are much the same way. You find yourself arriving on time for events. You are faithful to your Bible study and prayer, your attitude toward others is really good, and your follow through is right where it needs to be. Then something unexpected occurs, and your routine is thrown off for a few days. The next thing you know, your focus has shifted, and you realize that you are getting back into the old lifestyle habits once again. Well, the good news is that you don't have to stay there. You will have pitfalls, but the key is to always remain faithful to God because He promises to remain faithful to you.

God never gives up on you!

In order to feel good about myself, I have learned that I need to help others feel good about themselves. Share ideas that have helped you simplify your life with others. In the space below list ways that you can help others learn to simplify.

_____

_____

_____

When you see a friend that appears to be overwhelmed, frazzled, and weary, be transparent, and let them know that they are not alone. Be a support for someone in need. If you need to clean out a closet and you know someone that is in need of clothes, shoes, and purses, then help them out by giving your things to them. You will feel good when you see that you have helped someone else feel good about themselves. When you see that a friend needs some down time, offer to watch her children for a day. One day without any responsibilities can work wonders in the area of sanity! If you know a family that is struggling financially, invite them over for a meal, and send the leftovers home with them.

In the space below, write a prayer to God asking him to show you ways to help others feel good about themselves.

THOUGHT FOR THE DAY
When you cook in quantity for your own family, make an extra casserole to give away.

_____

_____

_____

When you take time to help others, you are obeying the two commandments that Jesus taught us. You are showing love to God and showing love to others, and in turn you will feel good about yourself.

In the space below, write the words to Matthew 22:37.

_____

_____

_____

_____

_____

People that live selfish lives are continuously frustrated because they are never satisfied. They always want more for themselves. People that live for God and others will find that they live a fulfilled life and learn to be content along life's way. I have discovered that no matter how hard I try I will never be able to please everyone. I can't make everyone happy, and I cannot change anyone except me. So I live my life to please God, and this gives me a peace that goes beyond anything I can put into words.

Mother Teresa was an inspiration to me. She lived a very simple life and understood the value of helping others. In her book entitled, _A Simple Faith_, one of her volunteers, Rupert, writes this, "The more you give the more you get. And all the time you're giving, loving, and helping, more is given to the world, more than we'd ever know from our one small step. It's like having a kind of empathy with the heart of the world."

ANYWAY

People are unreasonable, illogical, and self-centered,

LOVE THEM ANYWAY

If you do good, people will accuse you of selfish, ulterior motives,

DO GOOD ANYWAY

If you are successful, you win false friends and true enemies,

SUCCEED ANYWAY

The good you do will be forgotten tomorrow,

DO GOOD ANYWAY

Honesty and frankness make you vulnerable,

BE HONEST AND FRANK ANYWAY

What you spent years building may be destroyed overnight,

BUILD ANYWAY

People really need help but may attack you if you help them,

HELP PEOPLE ANYWAY

Give the world the best you have and you'll get kicked in the teeth,

GIVE THE WORLD THE BEST YOU'VE GOT ANYWAY.

*From a sign on the wall of Shishu Bhavan, the children's home in Calcuttta
Mother Teresa, Simple Faith*

DAY 4

SWEET DREAMS

When you first started thinking about working for a living, what did you want to do, and how has that brought you to where you are today? When I interview people for potential job opportunities, I ask the question that I just asked you. Remember when you were in grade school and you were asked to write a story about what you wanted to be when you grew up? What did you write about?

VERSES FOR THE DAY

"For I know the plans I have for you," says the Lord. "They are plans for good and not for disaster, to give you a future and a hope."
Jeremiah 29:11 (NLT)

O Lord, you have examined my heart and know everything about me.
Psalm 139:1 (NLT)

Now all glory to God, who is able, through his mighty power at work within us, to accomplish infinitely more than we might ask or think. Glory to him in the church and in Christ Jesus through all generations forever and ever! Amen.
Ephesians 3:20-21 (NLT)

"I am the true grapevine, and my Father is the gardener. He cuts off every branch of mine that doesn't produce fruit, and he prunes the branches that do bear fruit so they will produce even more. You have already been pruned and purified by the message I have given you. Remain in me, and I will remain in you. For a branch cannot produce fruit if it is severed from the vine, and you cannot be fruitful unless you remain in me. "Yes, I am the vine; you are the branches. Those who remain in me, and I in them, will produce much fruit. For apart from me you can do nothing.
John 15:1–5 (NLT)

When I was a young girl, my story would change from year to year. Even then it had some of the same elements throughout. When I was a very young girl, I wanted to be the first woman on the moon and a teacher. Then when I got a little older, I wanted to be the first woman President and a teacher. Then when I got into junior high and high school, I wanted to be a High School Band Director. At that point, I began to train musically to reach this goal. I was the Student Conductor for the Concert Band, from Junior High School through High School. I learned to play all of the woodwind instruments and could play some brass instruments as well. I assisted the High School Band Director with planning pre-game and half time formations, twirled the baton, participated in instrumental ensembles, and collegiate competitions. I was even chosen for the All-State High School Band at Florida State University. This was my dream. Then early in my adult life, I decided to change my goal and instead of teaching high school students, I wanted to become a college professor. I love music and have always enjoyed Music Theory. So I decided that I would teach Music Theory in such a way that students majoring in music would look forward to courses that I taught. Again, this was my dream. Did you catch the key word in the last sentence? My dream. In order to teach on a college level, one must acquire a master's degree. I married at a young age, became a mother at a young age, and then went to college. I did not receive my master's degree and realized early on that I needed to pursue a different career path.

I have never lost my love for music, and I have had the privilege of teaching music for over half of my adult life. In my current job I get to be around people that love music just as much as I do. Have my dreams come true?

God instilled a desire inside of me, and I believe He did this before I was born. I have always enjoyed teaching in some fashion. I also believe that God's dreams for my life far outweigh mine, and He knows what is best for me. He also knows what is best for you!

In the space below, write your answer to this question: When you first started thinking about working for a living, what did you want to do, and how has that brought you to where you are today?

_____

_____

_____

Early on in this study we talked about setting goals. Goals and dreams go hand in hand. It is important to seek God's guidance as you make plans. If you are still having trouble writing out your goals, then I suggest that you take some time to pull out old high school year books, or look at old pictures, and see what your main interests have been throughout your life.

In the space below, write about the things you love to do. These should be things that you would do even if you didn't get paid to do them.

_____

_____

_____

Do you have time to do the things you love? _____

In the space below, write a prayer to God asking him to show you the God size dreams that he has placed in your heart.

_____

_____

_____

THOUGHT FOR THE DAY
Help a friend who's going through something hard to take a moment and write down her blessings. Chances are she'll notice something and be uplifted.

YOU ARE NEVER TOO OLD TO START SOMETHING NEW!

You are never too old to start something new! Laura Ingalls Wilder was 64 when she wrote her first book of _Little House on the Prairie_. I know a man who in his late sixties wrote his first book. He has had a passion for hymns of the church for years. He has collected over four hundred hymnals from around the country and the world. He is so passionate about his new-found talent and already writing his second book. When he talks about his book, he has a glow about him that is truly from God. I have a friend that graduated from college at the age of 52. I taught beginner piano lessons to adults in their forties and fifties. I have known men in their thirties and forties that decided to go to Bible college in order to become ministers. These men were married with children. They uprooted their families and started as freshmen in college. I have a friend that graduated from college the same year that her son graduated from high school. I could go on and on, but I will simply repeat myself one more time... You are never too old to start something new!

Dear Heavenly
Father,
Thank you for
instilling God size
dreams in my
heart.
Help me to
simplify my life so
that I can better
serve you.
Give me guidance
and wisdom as I
go through this
day.
May I live my life
in a way that will
be pleasing to
you.
In your son's
name, I pray.
Amen.

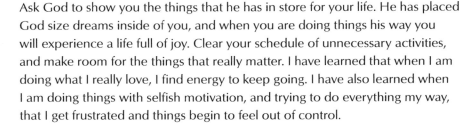

Ask God to show you the things that he has in store for your life. He has placed God size dreams inside of you, and when you are doing things his way you will experience a life full of joy. Clear your schedule of unnecessary activities, and make room for the things that really matter. I have learned that when I am doing what I really love, I find energy to keep going. I have also learned when I am doing things with selfish motivation, and trying to do everything my way, that I get frustrated and things begin to feel out of control.

I have decided to live the life out of every day and to dream God size dreams. My dreams were adequate and consisted of some of the things God had instilled in me. Now that I am living my life with God in the driver's seat, I love my life!

I still face temptations, struggles, and heartache. That is part of life. You will face temptations, struggles, and heartache too. I assure you that living your life with God will make those times of temptation, struggle, and heartache a whole lot easier.

Each day for years I have prayed this prayer:

Dear Heavenly Father,
Show me the things you want me to see today.
Reveal my sins to me and cleanse me of them.
Help me to dream God size dreams.
Use me today, however you see fit to use me.
Help me to find humor in this day.
Help me to show you how much I love you.
Help me to treat everyone with dignity and respect.
In your son's name, I pray.
Amen.

When you ask God to help you dream God size dreams, you will begin to see things around you in a different way. You will begin to see areas where you can use your God-given talents. Instead of asking what others can do for you, you will begin to ask what you can do for others.

There is a song that I love to teach children that includes the following lyrics:

> You are a Promise,
> You are a Possibility.
> You are a Promise with a capital P.
> You are a great big bundle of potentiality.
> And if you listen, you'll hear God's voice.
> And if you're trying, he'll help you make the right choices.
> You're a Promise to be anything He wants you to be!

You are a Promise! In the space below, write a prayer to God asking him to help you simplify in order to have time to follow your God size dreams.

_____

_____

_____

DAY 5
MAKING IT FUN

VERSES FOR THE DAY

This is the day the Lord has made. We will rejoice and be glad in it.
Psalm 118:24 (NLT)

Give thanks to the Lord, for he is good! His faithful love endures forever.
Psalm 118:1 (NLT)

Commit your actions to the Lord, and your plans will succeed.
Proverbs 16:3 (NLT)

For our earthly fathers disciplined us for a few years, doing the best they knew how. But God's discipline is always good for us, so that we might share in his holiness. No discipline is enjoyable while it is happening—it's painful! But afterward there will be a peaceful harvest of right living for those who are trained in this way. So take a new grip with your tired hands and strengthen your weak knees. Mark out a straight path for your feet so that those who are weak and lame will not fall but become strong.
Hebrews 12:10 -13 (NLT)

Are you having fun yet? Are you beginning to see life with a whole new approach?

My father used to say, "Sue Ann, life is way too short so don't allow yourself to be miserable." He was a very optimistic person, and his enthusiasm for life was contagious. There are days when it can be very difficult to take a positive approach, but starting your day off in God's word will allow you to see things in a better light.

What have you learned about yourself through this SIMPLIFY study?

_____

_____

_____

In the space below, list some of the habits that you have changed as a result of this study.

_____

_____

_____

_____

Are you finding more time for things in life that matter most? Learning to simplify your life is a work in progress. Remember you did not get in this shape overnight, and you can't fix it overnight. Keep your study guide handy, and refer to it when you feel yourself slipping back into a cluttered and unorganized state.

The Three Key Elements For a Simpler Life:

DAILY BIBLE STUDY, DAILY PRAYER, PERSONAL GOALS

You have come a long way in a short amount of time, and I am certain that good habits have been formed. Life really is too short to live in chaos all of the time. It is my prayer that you have realized that living a simplified life allows you to enjoy more time with your family and friends. Being on time for events allows you to receive the full benefit of the occasion, and you no longer have to wonder what you've missed. Cleaning up and cleaning out allows you to find things without wasting time and energy. There are many other areas of learned improvements that will enable you to experience a fulfilled life the way God intended. You simply need to stay focused on your goals.

In the space below, write a prayer to God asking him to show you ways that you can help others learn to simplify.

_____

_____

_____

_____

_____

Wow, time really does fly! We have come to the end of our lessons. Take time today to celebrate. Celebrate all that God has taught you through this study. Have a fun-filled day! If you can't think of anything fun to do, then check out the list on the next page. You deserve a break today! Have fun!

**THOUGHT
FOR THE DAY**

Enjoy yourself.
These are the
"good old days'
you're going to
miss in the years
ahead.

- Anonymous

**PRAYER FOR
THE DAY**

Dear Heavenly
Father,
Thank you for
loving me and
showing me a
simpler way of
life.
Help me to stay
focused in the
days ahead.
Show me the
things that you
want me to see.
Help me to
continue
to pursue a
simplified life that
is pleasing to you.
In your son's
name, I pray.
Amen.

- Call a friend on the spur of the moment, and go to a movie.
- Meet a friend in the wee hours of the morning for a walk.
- Volunteer at your local church for two hours.
- Attend a sporting event.
- Have a romantic evening with your hubby.
- Host a backyard barbeque.
- Ask someone to join you in pursuing a new hobby.
- Go for a drive through the countryside with someone special.
- Meet a friend for an early breakfast to catch up.
- Pack a picnic lunch, and take someone special to a surprise location.
- Greet everyone you meet today with a smile.
- Invite a close friend to shop with you for a new outfit.
- Surprise your children by stopping by an ice-cream shop on the way home from school.
- Kidnap someone you care about who's had a hard week. Use a bandanna as a blindfold and travel in a roundabout way to her favorite restaurant.
- Make a special certificate of achievement to celebrate your success in the Simplify study.
- Surprise someone in your family with a "just because I love you" gift.
- Pamper yourself with a manicure and pedicure.

As you celebrate this day, why not bake something for your friends and family to enjoy?

Here is a recipe that has been a family favorite at my house for years. It is delicious and easy to make.

TODAY'S RECIPE

SOUR CREAM POUND CAKE

1 box of yellow cake mix

¾ cup of oil

½ cup of sugar

4 eggs

1 cup of sour cream

1 tsp. Almond extract

1 tsp. Lemon extract

Pour all the above into a bowl and mix until fluffy. Flour and grease
Bundt cake pan. Preheat oven for 30 minutes at 350 degrees.
Bake cake for 40 minutes.

GROUP SESSION

WEEK 6

THE SECRET TO SIMPLIFY SUCCESS

I. In order to get the most out of _____, we must learn to _____.

Philippians 4:11-12
Not that I was ever in need, for I have _____ how to be _____
with whatever I _____. I know how to live on almost _____ or
with everything. I have learned the _____ of living in every situation,
whether it is with a full stomach or _____, with _____ or little.

II. To live a simplified lifestyle, I need to _____God.

Proverbs 3:5-6
_____ in the _____ with all your _____; do not depend on your
own understanding. _____ his will in all you do, and he will _____
you which path to take.

III. When I begin to waver, I need to _____ to my goals.

Jeremiah 29:11
"For I know the _____ I have for you," says the Lord. "They are _____
for _____ and not for disaster, to give you a _____ and a _____."

As we conclude this S I M P L I F Y Study, I pray that you will continue to
keep God first in all you do, take time for Bible study and prayer daily, love
God and love others. If you will do these things, you will have a simpler life.
I guarantee it!

SIMPLIFY

A Life Anchored in Purpose

GROUP SESSION LEADER'S GUIDE

GROUP SESSION LEADER'S GUIDE

Introduction:
SIMPLIFY is a six-week Bible study on ways to change habits, re-prioritize, set goals, and begin to experience a simpler way of life. It can be used for individual study or in a group setting. Why not invite your friends, neighbors, co-workers, or church group to come together for a weekly time of fun, fellowship, and encouragement?

Group Session Leader:
You do not need a long list of qualifications or years of teaching experience to lead **SIMPLIFY**. You need a heart prepared by God with availability and a willingness to facilitate. As the leader, you will not teach the material, you will simply help others learn for themselves.

Success as a facilitator depends on:
- A heart committed to leading and encouraging others in a pursuit to simplify.
- A commitment to complete this study.
- Faithfulness to each weekly meeting.

Before the Session:
1. Each week complete the daily lessons in the workbook.
2. Pray for each member of your group by name.
3. Pray for God's guidance as you prepare for each week's group session.
4. Arrange your room to meet the needs of your group. An intimate setting seems to work best.

During The Session: Start on time!
At the Introductory Session inform the members you plan to start promptly each week, and let them know arriving on time is one of the first steps to a simpler life.

Most of the women that will participate in this study are usually running late. Use incentives to encourage early arrival. How about a chest full of organizational "treasures?" Items such as calendars, highlighters, cosmetic bags, pens, journals, chip clips, and day planners. Let the members know that the Treasure Chest will be open 15 minutes before the start time, and will remain open until time to begin. If they arrive early or on time they can get something out of the Treasure Chest. Everyone likes to get a prize. I have used this incentive program and it works! Women that thought they could never arrive anywhere on time are now in the habit of arriving 15 minutes early and feel great about doing so.

SUGGESTED SCHEDULE:

1. Arrival Activity (10 min)

- Share prayer requests – remind the members to be brief and to the point.
- List requests as you receive them so that you can refer to them as you pray.
- Lead the group to pray for each request. Ask God to open the hearts and minds of every member present and for blessings throughout the session.

2. Review the Week's Scriptures and Questions (40 min.)

Start with the Introduction page for each week and begin asking the members to tell you which Bible verses meant the most to them throughout the week. Next, start with Day 1 and ask for brief and basic answers to the questions. This will allow you to confirm that the study content was received and understood.

Questions can be answered by anyone who feels comfortable sharing. Encourage participation, however, do not pressure members to share personal answers, but allow them the opportunity if desired. Ask them to be discreet; not to use names if and when they could be hurt by the discussion. Appropriate discussion of these questions is invaluable to the application of the unit. Be prepared to redirect if at any point the discussion becomes inappropriate. Pray for discretion and boldness to redirect if necessary.

3. Group Session Worksheets (15 min.)

The worksheet at the end of the lessons each week is to be filled out during this time period as a group. All scriptures used are from the New Living Translation, and the answers are provided in your Leader's Guide. The worksheet is to be used as a "wrap up" of the week's lessons and should serve as a tool of encouragement as well as a reminder of just how much God loves each member individually.

4. Conclusion of Session (5 min.)

- Give a brief introduction to next week's study and encourage members to complete their home study.
- Close with prayer. Since prayer requests were taken at the beginning of the session, refrain from asking for them again.

After The Session:

1. While the session is still fresh on your mind, immediately record the concerns of group members. Remember to pray for these concerns throughout the week.

2. Evaluate the session by asking yourself the following questions.
- Was I adequately prepared for today's session?
- Did I begin and end on time? If not, how can I use the time more wisely next session?
- Does anyone need extra encouragement this week? Remember to follow-up with a card or phone call.

I thank God for women like you who are committed to teaching, leading, and encouraging others through Bible study. God created each of us for a life anchored in simplicity, contentment, joy, and rest. Many women feel that every hour is a rush hour and the more they try and get organized, the more disorganized they get. They begin to feel their lives are out of control. Words such as "exhausted," "overwhelmed," and "frazzled" are used to describe their hectic lifestyles.

It is my prayer for you to receive guidance and direction from God as you help others discover there is no better, simpler plan for their lives than the one God has for them. God created each of us for a life anchored in simplicity, contentment, joy, and rest.

Sue Ann Cordell

GROUP SESSION

MOVE OUT THE CLUTTER AND MAKE ROOM FOR GOD

I.   For <u>EVERYTHING</u> there is a season, a <u>TIME</u> for every activity under
     heaven. Ecclesiastes 3:1

     The time to simplify is <u>NOW</u>. The time to get rid of the <u>CLUTTER</u> is now.

     Definition of closet – n. a small cabinet, compartment or room for storage.
     Definition of clean – adj. Free from impurities, dirt, or contamination; neat.

II. <u>GREED</u> is a selfish desire to acquire more than one needs or deserves. A
     person that is greedy is never satisfied with what they have. They always
     want more. They are so busy making money so they can have more stuff,
     bigger houses, better cars, get a better job, and on and on it goes.

     Problem: Little or no time for God, family, or friends.

III. <u>GUILT</u> is knowing that you have done something wrong and you feel the
     need to hide it. Women tend to feel <u>UNNECESSARY</u> guilt.

     "But those who do what is <u>RIGHT</u> come to the light so others can see that
     they are doing what <u>GOD</u> wants."" John 3:21.

<u>GOSSIP</u> is often malicious talk; a person who spreads sensational or
     intimate facts.

     So be careful how you <u>LIVE</u>, Don't live like fools, but like those who are
     <u>WISE</u>. Ephesians 5:15

GROUP SESSION
ANSWERS - WEEK 2

WHEN THE TIME IS RIGHT - GIVE IT AWAY

I.   Imitate God, therefore, in everything you do, because <u>YOU</u> are his dear <u>CHILDREN</u>. Live a life filled with love, following the <u>EXAMPLE</u> of Christ. He <u>LOVED</u> us and offered himself as a sacrifice for us, a pleasing <u>AROMA</u> to God. Ephesians 5:1-2 (NLT)

II.   <u>EXPERIENCE</u> - Give it away only when asked. When giving it away, you make room for more. Ask God to give you wisdom to know when to speak and when to lead by <u>EXAMPLE</u>.

III. <u>MEMORIES</u> - Whether we like it or not, we are creating <u>MEMORIES</u> for those that we influence. When giving these away, you make room for more.

IV.   <u>ENCOURAGEMENT</u> - It's never too late to offer this through <u>PHONE CALLS</u>, cards, kind words and smiles. When giving this away, you are making room for more opportunities.

V.   To those who use well what they are <u>GIVEN</u>, even more will be given, and they will have an abundance. But from those who do nothing, even what <u>LITTLE</u> they have will be taken <u>AWAY</u>. Matthew 25:29 (NLT)

GROUP SESSION

ANSWERS - WEEK 3

MOVE OUT THE CLOUDS AND MAKE ROOM FOR SUNLIGHT

I.   God wants to <u>BLESS</u> you and give you his <u>BEST</u>.

     How <u>GREAT</u> is the goodness you have stored up for those who <u>FEAR</u> you. You lavish it on those who come to you for <u>PROTECTION</u>, <u>BLESSING</u> them before the watching <u>WORLD</u>. Psalm 31:19

II. Even when your situation seems <u>ENORMOUS</u>, <u>OVERWHELMING</u>, or <u>SCARY</u>, don't give up without even trying!

     Let your favor <u>SHINE</u> on your servant. In your <u>UNFAILING</u> love, rescue me. Psalm 31:16

III. Remember that God is <u>ALWAYS</u> with <u>YOU</u>!

     Once I was young, and now I am <u>OLD</u>. Yet I have never seen the godly abandoned, or their children begging for <u>BREAD</u>. Psalm 37:25

How do you see the world? How do you see the circumstances around you? Do you look at life through rose colored glasses or are you an active member of the Doom and Gloom Club? Do you feel defeated before the battle even begins?

With God's help, you can conquer every fear, see things through His eyes, and resign from the Doom and Gloom Club! He will go with you right into the fog and bring you into the bright sunshine!

For I can do <u>EVERYTHING</u> through Christ, who gives me <u>STRENGTH</u>. Philippians 4:13

GROUP SESSION

ANSWERS - WEEK 4

CLEAR THE ROOM – THE REAL ME IS COMING THROUGH!

I.   Being <u>TRANSPARENT</u> is an important step toward simplifying your <u>LIFE</u>. Realizing and admitting that <u>EVERYTHING</u> that is good in your life has come from <u>GOD</u> helps you let go of the <u>CONTROL</u> that belongs to Him.

Psalm 16:2
I said to the Lord, "You are my <u>MASTER</u>! Every <u>GOOD</u> thing I have comes from <u>YOU</u>."

II. God loves you with an <u>UNFAILING</u> love and considers you to be the <u>APPLE</u> of his eye!

Psalm 17:8
Guard me as you would <u>GUARD</u> your own <u>EYES</u>. Hide me in the shadow of your <u>WINGS</u>.

III. Accepting God's love and loving Him in return will enable you to look at things <u>DIFFERENTLY</u>. Loving <u>GOD</u> and loving <u>OTHERS</u> are the two main principles of a <u>CHRISTIAN</u> life.

Matthew 22:37-40
Jesus replied, "'You must <u>LOVE</u> the Lord your God with all your <u>HEART</u>, all your <u>SOUL</u>, and all your <u>MIND</u>.' This is the first and greatest commandment. A second is equally <u>IMPORTANT</u>: 'Love your neighbor as <u>YOURSELF</u>.' The entire law and all the <u>DEMANDS</u> of the prophets are based on these two commandments."

GROUP SESSION

SHHH – I'M TRYING TO REST!

I.   There is no need to <u>WORRY</u>. God is in <u>CONTROL</u>.
     He provides <u>REST</u> for the <u>WEARY</u> and <u>STRENGTH</u> for his people.

     Psalm 29:10 -11
     The Lord <u>RULES</u> over the floodwaters.
     The <u>LORD</u> reigns as king <u>FOREVER</u>. The Lord gives his <u>PEOPLE</u> strength.
     The Lord <u>BLESSES</u> them with peace.

II. Without <u>REST</u> we will become ineffective in our <u>LIFE</u>. If <u>MOMMA</u> ain't
     happy, ain't <u>NOBODY</u> happy! Sometimes the best thing for us is a <u>NAP</u>!

     Isaiah 40:30
     Even youths will become <u>WEAK</u> and <u>TIRED</u>, and young men will fall in
     exhaustion.

III. Psalm 23:2-3
     He lets me <u>REST</u> in green meadows; he leads me beside <u>PEACEFUL</u>
     streams He <u>RENEWS</u> my <u>STRENGTH</u>. He guides me along right paths,
     bringing <u>HONOR</u> to his name.

     Spending quiet time with God is an important step in simplifying your life.
     He provides rest for the weary, strength for each day, and a peace that
     surpasses our understanding.

GROUP SESSION

ANSWERS - WEEK 6

THE SECRET TO SIMPLIFY SUCCESS

I. In order to get the most out of <u>LIFE</u>, we must learn to <u>SIMPLIFY</u>.

Philippians 4:11-12
Not that I was ever in need, for I have <u>LEARNED</u> how to be <u>CONTENT</u> with whatever I <u>HAVE</u>. I know how to live on almost <u>NOTHING</u> or with everything. I have learned the <u>SECRET</u> of living in every situation, whether it is with a full stomach or <u>EMPTY</u>, with <u>PLENTY</u> or little.

II. To live a simplified lifestyle, I need to <u>TRUST</u> God.

Proverbs 3:5-6
<u>Trust</u> in the <u>LORD</u> with all your <u>HEART</u>; do not depend on your own understanding. <u>SEEK</u> his will in all you do, and he will <u>SHOW</u> you which path to take.

III. When I begin to waver, I need to <u>RE-COMMIT</u> to my goals.

Jeremiah 29:11
"For I know the <u>PLANS</u> I have for you," says the Lord. "They are <u>PLANS</u> for <u>GOOD</u> and not for disaster, to give you a <u>FUTURE</u> and a <u>HOPE</u>."

As we conclude this S I M P L I F Y Study, I pray that you will continue to keep God first in all you do, take time for Bible study and prayer daily, love God and love others. If you will do these things, you will have a simpler life. I guarantee it!

NOTES

NOTES

NOTES

12483665R00085

Made in the USA
Charleston, SC
08 May 2012